Karen Brown's
England
Charming Bed & Breakfasts

Written by
JUNE BROWN

Illustrations by Barbara Tapp
Cover Painting by Jann Pollard

Karen Brown's Guides, San Mateo, California

Karen Brown Titles

Austria: Charming Inns & Itineraries
California: Charming Inns & Itineraries
England: Charming Bed & Breakfasts
England, Wales & Scotland: Charming Hotels & Itineraries
France: Charming Bed & Breakfasts
France: Charming Inns & Itineraries
Germany: Charming Inns & Itineraries
Ireland: Charming Inns & Itineraries
Italy: Charming Bed & Breakfasts
Italy: Charming Inns & Itineraries
Mexico: Charming Inns & Itineraries*
Mid-Atlantic: Charming Inns & Itineraries
New England: Charming Inns & Itineraries
Pacific Northwest: Charming Inns & Itineraries*
Portugal: Charming Inns & Itineraries
Spain: Charming Inns & Itineraries
Switzerland: Charming Inns & Itineraries

*Now on our website, *www.karenbrown.com*, soon to be in print

Dedicated with All My Love
to My Parents
Gladys & George

Editors: Anthony Brown, Karen Brown, June Brown, Clare Brown, Iris Sandilands, Lorena Aburto Ramirez.

Illustrations: Barbara Tapp; Cover painting: Jann Pollard; Web designer: Lynn Upthagrove.

Maps: Susanne Lau Alloway—Greenleaf Design & Graphics; Inside cover photo: W. Russell Ohlson.

Copyright © 2002 by Karen Brown's Guides.

Distributed by Fodor's Travel Publications, Inc., 280 Park Avenue, New York, NY 10017, USA.

Distributed in Canada by Random House Canada, 2775 Matheson Boulevard. East, Mississauga, Ontario, Canada L4W 4P7, phone: (905) 624 0672, fax: (905) 624 6217.

Distributed in the United Kingdom, Ireland and Europe by Random House UK, 20 Vauxhall Bridge Road, London, SW1V 2SA, England, phone: 44 20 7840 4000, fax: 44 20 7840 8406.

Distributed in Australia by Random House Australia, 20 Alfred Street, Milsons Point, Sydney NSW 2061, Australia, phone: 61 2 9954 9966, fax: 61 2 9954 4562.

Distributed in New Zealand by Random House New Zealand, 18 Poland Road, Glenfield, Auckland, New Zealand, phone: 64 9 444 7197, fax: 64 9 444 7524.

Distributed in South Africa by Random House South Africa, Endulani, East Wing, 5A Jubilee Road, Parktown 2193, South Africa, phone: 27 11 484 3538, fax: 27 11 484 6180.

A catalog record for this book is available from the British Library.

ISSN 1534-4630

Contents

Introduction

England: Charming Bed & Breakfasts describes special accommodations in tranquil countryside locations, picturesque villages, historic towns, and a selection of interesting cities beyond London. Interspersed with thatched cottages and grand ancestral manors are traditional pubs and guesthouses—all offering wholehearted hospitality in charming surroundings. Every place to stay is one that we have seen and enjoyed—our personal recommendation. We sincerely believe that where you lay your head each night makes the difference between a good and a great vacation. Please supplement this book with the Karen Brown website (*www.karenbrown.com*). Our site contains post-press updates on our guides and a wealth of information for planning your holiday, and is a one-stop shop for our guides and Michelin maps. A great many of the properties in this guide are featured there (their web addresses are on their description pages) with photos and direct links to their email and their own websites. If you prefer to travel the hotel route or are looking for itinerary suggestions, we trust you'll find just what you need in our companion guide, *England, Wales & Scotland: Charming Hotels & Itineraries*.

About Bed & Breakfast Travel

Every place to stay in this book has a different approach to bed and breakfast. Some households are very informal, some welcome children, and others invite you to sample gracious living, cocktails in the drawing room, billiards after dinner, and croquet on the lawn. The one thing that they have in common is a warmth of welcome. We have tried to be candid and honest in our appraisals and tried to convey each listing's special flavor so that you know what to expect and will not be disappointed. To help you appreciate and understand what to expect when staying at places in this guide, the following pointers are given in alphabetical order, not order of importance.

ANIMALS

Even if animals are not mentioned in the write-up, the chances are that there are friendly, tail-wagging dogs and sleek cats as visible members of the families. Many listings accept their guests' pets.

ARRIVAL AND DEPARTURE

Always discuss your time of arrival—hosts usually expect you to arrive around 6 pm. If you are going to arrive late or early, be certain to telephone your host. You are generally expected to leave by 10 on the morning of your departure. By and large, you are not expected to be on the premises during the day.

BATHROOMS

Not all listings have en-suite bathrooms leading from the bedrooms. Several have private bathrooms, which means that your facilities are located down the hall.

BEDROOMS

Beds are often made with duvets (down comforters) instead of the more traditional blankets and sheets. A double room has one double bed, a twin room has two single beds, and a family room contains one or more single beds in addition to a double bed. Zip and link beds are very popular: these are twin beds that can be zipped together (linked) to form an American queen-sized bed. American king and queen beds are not found very often.

CHILDREN

Places that welcome children state "Children welcome." The majority of listings in this guide do not "welcome" children but find they become tolerable at different ages over 5 or, more often than not, over 12. Some places simply do not accept children and the listing notes "Children not accepted." However, these indications of children's acceptability are not cast in stone, so, for example, if you have your heart set on staying at a listing that accepts children over 12, and you have an 8-year-old, call them, explain your situation, and they may well take you. Ideally, we would like to see all listings welcoming children and all parents remembering that they are staying in a home and doing their bit by making sure that children do not run wild.

CHRISTMAS

Several places offer Christmas getaways. If the information section indicates that the listing is open during the Christmas season, there is a very good chance that it offers a festive Christmas package.

CREDIT CARDS

Many bed and breakfasts in this guide do not accept plastic payment. To pay in cash, an increasingly popular and convenient way to obtain pounds sterling is simply to use your bankcard at an ATM machine. You pay a fixed fee for this but, depending on the amount you withdraw, it is usually less than the percentage-based fee charged to exchange currency or travelers' checks. If payment by credit card is accepted, it is indicated using the terms AX—American Express, MC—MasterCard, VS—Visa, or simply, all major.

DIRECTIONS

We give concise driving directions to guide you to the listing, which is often in a more out-of-the-way place than the town or village in the address. We would be very grateful if you would let us know of cases where our directions have proved inadequate.

ELECTRICITY

The voltage is 240. Most bathrooms have razor points (American-style) for 110 volts. It is recommended that overseas visitors take only dual-voltage appliances and a kit of electrical plug adapters. Often your host can loan you a hairdryer or an iron.

HANDICAP FACILITIES

At the back of the book we list all the places to stay that have ground-floor rooms or rooms specially equipped for the handicapped. Please discuss your requirements when you call your chosen place to stay to see if they have accommodation that is suitable for you.

MAPS

At the back of the book are a key map and six regional maps of England showing the location of the town or village nearest the lodging. To make it easier for you, we have divided each location map into a grid of four parts—a, b, c, and d—as indicated on each map's key. The pertinent regional map number is given at the right on the top line of each bed and breakfast's description. Our maps can be cross-referenced with those in our companion guide, *England, Wales & Scotland: Charming Hotels & Itineraries.* These maps are drawn by an artist and are not intended to replace commercial maps: our suggestion is that you purchase a large-scale road atlas of England where an inch equals 10 miles. We use the Michelin Tourist and Motoring Atlas of Great Britain–1122, which you can purchase from our website, *www.karenbrown.com.*

MEALS

Prices quoted always include breakfast. Breakfast is most likely to be juice, a choice of porridge (oatmeal) or cereal, followed by a plate of egg, bacon, sausage, tomatoes, and mushrooms completed by toast, marmalade, and jams—all accompanied by tea or coffee. A great many places offer evening meals, which should be requested at the time you make your reservation. You cannot expect to arrive at a bed and breakfast and receive dinner if you have not made reservations for it several days in advance. At some homes the social occasion of guests and host gathered around the dining-room table for an evening dinner party is a large part of the overall experience and many of these types of listings expect their guests to dine in. Places that do not offer evening meals are always happy to make recommendations at nearby pubs or restaurants.

RATES

Rates are those quoted to us for the 2002 summer season. We have tried to standardize rates by quoting the 2002 per person bed-and-breakfast rate based on two people occupying a room. Not all places conform, so where dinner is included we have stated this in the listing. Prices are always quoted to include breakfast, Value Added Tax (VAT), and service (if these are applicable). Please use the figures printed as a guideline and be certain to ask what the rate is at the time of booking. Prices for a single are usually higher than the per-person rates and prices for a family room are sometimes lower. Many listings offer special terms, below their normal prices, for "short breaks" of two or more nights. In several places suites are available at higher prices.

RESERVATIONS

When making your reservations, be sure to identify yourself as a "Karen Brown traveler." The proprietors appreciate your visit, value their inclusion in our guide, and frequently tell us they take special care of our readers, and many offer special rates to Karen Brown members (visit our website at *www.karenbrown.com*). We hear over and over again that the people who use our guides are such wonderful guests!

It is important to understand that once reservations for accommodation are confirmed, whether verbally, by phone or in writing, you are under contract. This means that the proprietor is obligated to provide the accommodation that was promised and that you are obligated to pay for it. If you cannot take up your accommodation, you are liable for a portion of the accommodation charges plus your deposit. (If you have to cancel your reservation, do so as soon as possible so that the proprietor can attempt to re-let your room, in which case you are liable only for the re-let fee or the deposit.) Although some proprietors do not strictly enforce a cancellation policy many, particularly the smaller properties in our book, simply cannot afford not to do so. Similarly many airline tickets cannot be changed or refunded without penalty. We recommend insurance to cover these types of additional expenses arising from cancellation due to unforeseen circumstances. A link on our website (*www.karenbrown.com*) will connect you to Access America, which offers a variety of insurance policies to fit your needs.

There are several options for making reservations:

EMAIL: This is our preferred way of making a reservation. If the bed and breakfast is on our website, we have included their email address in the listing and added a direct link on their Karen Brown web page. (Always spell out the month as the English reverse the American month/day numbering system.)

FAX: If you have access to a fax machine, this is a very quick way to reach a hotel/bed and breakfast. If the place to stay has a fax, we have included the number. (See comment under email about spelling out the month.)

LETTER: If you write for reservations, you will usually receive back your confirmation and a map. You should then send your deposit. (See comment under email about spelling out the month.)

TELEPHONE: By telephoning you have your answer immediately, so if space is not available, you can then decide on an alternative. If calling from the United States, allow for the time difference (England is five hours ahead of New York) so that you can call during their business day. Dial 011 (the international code), 44 (England's code), then the city code (dropping the 0) and the telephone number.

SIGHTSEEING

Since few countries have as much sightseeing to offer in such a concentrated space as England, we have tried to mention major attractions near each lodging to encourage you to spend several nights in each location. Within a few miles of every listing there are places of interest to visit and explore: lofty cathedrals, quaint churches, museums, and grand country houses.

SMOKING

Nearly all listings forbid smoking either in the bedrooms or public rooms. Some allow no smoking at all, in which case we state "No-smoking house." Ask about smoking policies if this is important to you—best to be forewarned rather than frustrated.

SOCIALIZING

We have tried to indicate the degree of socializing that is included in your stay as some hosts treat their guests like visiting friends and relatives, hosting cocktails, eating with them around the dining table, and joining them for coffee after dinner (the difference being that friends and relatives do not receive a bill at the end of their stay).

WEBSITE

Please visit the Karen Brown website (*www.karenbrown.com*) in conjunction with this book. It provides comments and discoveries from you, our readers, information on our latest finds, post-press updates, the opportunity to purchase goods and services that we recommend (rail tickets, car rental, travel insurance), and one-stop shopping for our guides and associated maps. Most of our favorite places to stay are featured on our website (their web addresses are on their description pages in this book) with color photos and, through direct links to their own websites, even more information. For the properties not participating in our online booking program, you can e-mail them directly, making reservations a breeze.

About England

DRIVING

Just about the time overseas visitors board their return flight home, they will have adjusted to driving on the "right" side, which is the left side in England. You must contend with such things as roundabouts (circular intersections); flyovers (overpasses); ring roads (peripheral roads whose purpose is to bypass city traffic); lorries (trucks); laybys (turnouts); boots (trunks); and bonnets (hoods). Pedestrians are permitted to cross the road anywhere and always have the right of way. Seat belts must be worn at all times.

Motorways: The letter "M" precedes these convenient routes to cover long distances. With three or more lanes of traffic either side of a central divider, you should stay in the left-hand lane except for passing. Motorway exits are numbered and correspond to numbering on major road maps. Service areas supply petrol (gas), cafeterias, and "bathrooms" (the word "bathroom" is used in the American sense—in Britain "bathroom" means a room with a shower or bathtub, not a toilet: "loo" is the most commonly used term for an American bathroom).

"A" Roads: The letter "A" precedes the road number. All major roads fall into this category. They vary from three lanes either side of a dividing barrier to single carriageways with an unbroken white line in the middle indicating that passing is not permitted. These roads have the rather alarming habit of changing abruptly from dual to single carriageway.

"B" Roads and Country Roads: The letter "B" preceding the road number or the lack of any lettering or numbering indicates that the road belongs to the maze of country roads that crisscross Britain. These are the roads for people who have the luxury of time to enjoy the scenery en route. Arm yourself with a good map (although getting lost is part of the fun). Driving these narrow roads is terrifying at first but exhilarating after a while. Meandering down these roads, you can expect to spend time crawling behind a tractor or cows being herded to the farmyard. Some lanes are so narrow that there is room for only one car.

DRIVING–CAR RENTAL

Readers frequently ask our advice on car rental companies. We always use Auto Europe, a car rental broker that works with the major car rental companies to find the lowest possible price. They also offer motor homes and chauffeur services. Auto Europe's toll-free phone service from every European country connects you to their U.S.-based, 24-hour reservation center (ask for the card with European phone numbers to be sent to you). Auto Europe offers our readers a 5% discount, and occasionally free upgrades. Be sure to use the Karen Brown ID number 99006187 to receive your discount and any special offers. You can make your own reservations online via our website, *www.karenbrown.com* (select Auto Europe from the home page), or by phone (800-223-5555).

INFORMATION

The British Tourist Authority is an invaluable source of information. You can visit their website at *www.visitbritain.org*. Its major offices are located as follows:

AUSTRALIA–SYDNEY: BTA, Level 16, Gateway, 1 Macquarie Place, Sydney NWS 2000, tel: (02) 9377-4400, fax: (02) 9377-4499

CANADA–TORONTO: BTA, 5915 Airport Road, Suite 120, Mississauga, Ontario L4V 1T1, tel: (888) VISITUK

FRANCE–PARIS: BTA, Maison de la Grand Bretagne, 19 Rue des Mathurins, 75009 Paris, tel: (1) 4451-5620, fax: (1) 4451-5621

GERMANY–FRANKFURT: BTA, Westendstrasse 16-22, 60325 Frankfurt, tel: (069) 97 112-446, fax: (069) 97 112-444

NEW ZEALAND–AUCKLAND: BTA, Suite 305, 17th Floor, Fay Richwhite Building, 151 Queen Street, Auckland 1, tel: (09) 303-1446, fax: (09) 377-6965

USA–CHICAGO: BTA, 625 North Michigan Avenue, Suite 1001, Chicago, IL 60611—walk-in inquiries only

USA–NEW YORK: BTA, 551 Fifth Avenue, Suite 701, New York, NY 10176, tel: (800) 462-2748, email: travelinfo@bta.org.uk

If you need additional information while you are in Britain, there are more than 700 official Tourist Information Centres identified by a blue-and-white letter "I" and "Tourist Information" signs. Many information centers will make reservations for local accommodation and larger ones will "book a bed ahead" in a different locality.

In London at the British Visitor Centre at 1 Regent Street, London SW1Y 4PQ (near Piccadilly Circus tube station) you can book a room, hire a car, or pay for a coach tour or theatre tickets. It is open 9 am to 6:30 pm, Monday to Friday; 10 am to 4 pm Saturday and Sunday, with extended hours from mid-May to September.

PUBS

Pubs are a British institution. Traditional pubs with inviting names such as the Red Lion, Wheatsheaf, and King's Arms are found at the heart of every village. Not only are they a great place to meet the locals over a pint or a game of dominoes or darts, but they offer an inviting place to dine. Food served in the bar enables you to enjoy an inexpensive meal while sipping your drink in convivial surroundings. Bar meals range from a bowl of soup to a delicious cooked dinner. Many pubs have dining rooms that serve more elaborate fare in equally convivial but more sophisticated surroundings. The key to success when dining at a pub is to obtain a recommendation from where you are staying that night—your host is always happy to assist you.

SHOPPING

Non-EU members can reclaim the VAT (Value Added Tax) that they pay on the goods they purchase. Not all stores participate in the refund scheme and there is often a minimum purchase price. Stores that do participate will ask to see your passport before completing the VAT form. This form must be presented *with the goods* to the customs officer at the point of departure from Britain within three months of purchase. The customs officer will certify the form. After having the receipts validated by customs you can receive a refund in cash from the tax-free refund counter. Alternatively, you can mail your validated receipts to the store where you bought the goods. The store will then send you a check in sterling for the refund.

SIGHTSEEING

There is so much to see in every little nook and cranny of England: cottage gardens, Roman ruins, stately homes, thatched villages, ancient castles, Norman churches, smugglers' inns, bluebell woods, historic manors, museums on every subject. All set in a land that moves from wild moorland to verdant farmland, woodland to meadow, vast sandy beaches to rugged cliffs. Most sightseeing venues operate a summer and a winter opening schedule, the changeover occurring around late March/early April and late October/early November. Before you embark on an excursion, check the dates and hours of opening. The British Tourist Authority is an invaluable resource for what to see and do in an area. Our companion guide, *England, Wales & Scotland: Charming Hotels & Itineraries,* includes countryside driving itineraries that are useful in helping you plan your holiday.

WEATHER

Britain has a tendency to be moist at all times of the year. The cold in winter is rarely severe; however, the farther north you go, the greater the possibility of being snowed in. Spring can be wet, but it is a lovely time to travel—the summer crowds have not descended, daffodils and bluebells fill the woodlands, and the hedgerows are full of wildflowers. Summer offers the best chance of sunshine, but also the largest crowds. Schools are usually closed the last two weeks of July and all of August, so this is the time when most families take their summer holidays. Travel is especially hectic on the weekends in summer—try to avoid major routes and airports at these times. Autumn is also an ideal touring time. The weather tends to be drier than in spring and the woodlands are decked in their golden autumn finery.

Bed & Breakfast Descriptions

The Benedictine monks chose a magnificent site high on a hill overlooking the sea to found their Abbey of St. Peter in 1024. Despite having been sacked by Henry VIII and burned by Cromwell, a lot of the monastic settlement remains: the church, the magnificent swannery, an enormous thatched tithe barn, a ruined watermill, and, most importantly, the infirmary. Now home to the Cookes, the infirmary was originally a resting place for visitors, evolving over the years into a farmhouse and now a welcoming guesthouse and tea room. Pink chairs with tables topped with pink cloths are set around the giant inglenook fireplace in the old kitchen. Breakfast and lunch are served here or, on warm summer days, under the vine-covered arbor or on the lawn overlooking the barn. Bedrooms range in size from a spacious suite with a sitting room and separate bedroom to a cottagey little room set beneath the eaves and reached by a narrow staircase. The adjacent tithe barn contains interesting exhibits while the farm with its array of animals is a great attraction, as is the nearby swannery with its vast colony of swans. Abbotsbury is a delightful village of thatched houses very typical of those found just a short drive away in Hardy country, a favorite destination for visitors. *Directions*: Abbotsbury is midway between Weymouth and Bridport on the B3157. In Abbotsbury turn towards the sea (signposted The Swannery) and Abbey House is on your left after 100 yards.

ABBEY HOUSE
Owners: Maureen & Jonathan Cooke
Church Street
Abbotsbury
Dorset DT3 4JJ, England
Tel: (01305) 871330, Fax: (01305) 871088
Email: info@theabbeyhouse.co.uk
5 rooms
£30–£32.50 per person
Open all year, Credit cards: none
Children welcome, No-smoking house
www.karenbrown.com/england/abbey.html

Munden House is a little gem surrounded by peaceful Dorset countryside. The house was a complex of stone cottages built before 1700, converted to a farmhouse in the 19th century, and totally remodeled by Sylvia and Joe Benjamin at the end of the 20th century. It gave them a chance to show what they could do using their experience in designing private homes and interiors in the United States for 14 years. The resulting picturesque cottage complex is captivating. Relax and unwind in the stylishly decorated drawing room, enjoy breakfast under the soaring beams in the dining room, and visit one of the local pubs for dinner. Bedrooms are very nicely appointed. If you have children or want to stay for several days, opt for the studio suite with its own kitchenette and shower room. Just down the lane is an old-fashioned working bakery so you can always buy fresh rolls for picnics. Guests often visit the old port of Lyme Regis where Jane Austen wrote *Persuasion*, while Thomas Hardy fans head for his thatched home in Higher Bockingham. Lovers of quaint villages are spoilt for choice around here though Cerne Abbas has the added attraction of a 180-ft-high club-wielding giant carved into the hillside above it. Sherborne has some lovely golden-stone buildings, an abbey, and a castle. *Directions:* From Sherborne take the A352 towards Dorchester for 1 mile to the A3030 to Sturminster Newton. After 2 miles pass Alweston Post Office on the right and take the next tiny lane (Munden Lane). Munden House is the second building on the right.

MUNDEN HOUSE
Owners: Sylvia & Joe Benjamin
Alweston, Sherborne
Dorset DT9 5HU, England
Tel: (01963) 23150, Fax: (01963) 23153
Email: sylvia@mundonhouse.demon.co.uk
7 rooms
£32.50–£42.50 per person
Open all year, Credit cards: MC, VS
Children welcome in studio, No-smoking house
www.karenbrown.com/england/munden.html

Pam and David Veen run this impressive house, built as a vicarage in 1869, as a small hotel, providing a centrally located, comfortable, hospitable base for exploring the Lake District. Pamela decorated the house with antiques and bric-a-brac, creating interesting corners to relax and enjoy the tranquility that permeates this lovely old building. Most of the bedrooms have antique or four-poster beds with views across the river to the distant mountains. All have antique pictures and porcelain, crisp white sheets, and patchwork quilts. Accommodation can be taken on a bed-and-breakfast basis, but guests usually opt to include dinner because Pamela makes every effort to make this meal a special occasion. Grey Friar Lodge is just a short distance from the bustling center of Ambleside. Whether you explore Lakeland by car or on foot, you will find the scenery glorious: in spring the famous daffodils bloom, while in autumn the bracken and leaves turn a crisp, golden brown. At nearby Grasmere are Rydal Mount and Dove Cottage, poet William Wordsworth's homes. Hawkshead has a museum honoring Beatrix Potter and in Near Sawrey you can visit her home, Hill Top Farm, where she dreamed up such endearing characters as Mrs. Tiggy Winkle and the Flopsy Bunnies. *Directions:* Grey Friar Lodge is 1 mile west of Ambleside on the A593 (Coniston road), midway between Ambleside and Skelwith Bridge.

GREY FRIAR LODGE
Owners: Pam & David Veen
Clappersgate, Ambleside
Cumbria LA22 9NE, England
Tel & fax: (015394) 33158
Email: greyfriar@veen.freeserve.co.uk
8 rooms
£26–£44 per person, dinner from £19.50
Open Feb to mid-Dec
Credit cards: MC, VS
Children over 12, No-smoking house
www.karenbrown.com/england/greyfriarlodge.html

Magnificent sky-wide sunsets over the Howardian Hills are the order of the day from Shallowdale House. This substantial 1960s home built on a sheltered south-facing slope offers restorative countryside views through picture windows over fields of sheep, cattle, and horses to the distant hills. This lovely setting is matched by the hospitality, food, and comfort offered by Phillip Gill and Anton van der Horst. They welcome you with tea and homemade cakes just to whet your appetite for the candlelit dinner that follows several hours later. Menus are planned around what is fresh and local, with Anton and Phillip sharing the cooking and Anton taking care of guests in the dining room. Slip into utter relaxation in the drawing room where the comfortable scene is watched over by an unusual Friesland farmhouse wall clock from Anton's native Holland. Upstairs, two especially large, airy rooms are found at either end of the house, with a smaller double room in between with its bathroom across the hall. Guests can have lots of privacy but if they prefer, Anton and Phillip are always on hand to plan day trips with suggestions for lunch at their favorite haunts. Closer at hand lie the ruins of Rievaulx and Byland abbeys and the grand formality of the Howard family home, Castle Howard. *Directions:* From Thirsk take the A19 south towards York and then the "caravan route avoiding Sutton Bank" via Coxwold and Byland Abbey. Shallowdale House is on the left just before you enter the village.

SHALLOWDALE HOUSE
Owners: Phillip Gill & Anton van der Horst
West End, Ampleforth
North Yorkshire YO62 4DY, England
Tel: (01439) 788325, Fax: (01439) 788885
Email: stay@shallowdalehouse.demon.co.uk
3 rooms
£32.50–£40 per person, dinner £22.50
Closed Christmas & New Year, Credit cards: MC, VS
Children over 12, No-smoking house
www.karenbrown.com/england/shallowdale.html

The Barns is a comfortable spot to break a long journey between London and Edinburgh via the A1. It is also well located as a base from which to explore the Newark Antique Fairs, the Hemswell Antique Centre, or, on a longer visit, to explore Nottinghamshire. This county is famous not only for the exploits of Robin Hood, but also as the area where the Pilgrim Fathers formed their separatist church before setting sail for America and establishing a new colony. The Barns was very tastefully converted from the hay and tractor barns of the next-door farm, and behind its red-brick façade all is spick-and-span. Comfortable chairs are drawn round the fire in the cozy little sitting room where guests can enjoy a complimentary glass of whisky or sherry. In the spacious breakfast room the tables are topped with linen cloths neatly laid for breakfast. The bedrooms are immaculate, with rooms 1 and 5 being the most spacious. A small refrigerator is placed on the upstairs landing for guests to store their picnic supplies. A pleasant drive through Sherwood Forest brings you to the visitors' center, which has an exhibition on Robin Hood and his merry band and offers maps guiding you through ancient oak trees to his former hideaways. Clumber Park near Sherwood Forest is noted for its main driveway planted with over 1,296 lime trees. *Directions:* From the south take the A1 north to the A57 (Worksop) roundabout, make a U turn and go south on the A1. Take the first left, on the B6420, towards Retford. The Barns is on the left after 2 miles.

THE BARNS
Owners: Mary & Harry Kay
Morton Farm
Babworth, Retford
Nottinghamshire DN22 8HA, England
Tel: (01777) 706336, Fax: (01777) 709773
Email: harry@thebarns.fsbusiness.co.uk
6 rooms
£24–£30 per person
Open all year, Credit cards: all major
Children welcome, No-smoking house
www.karenbrown.com/england/thebarns.html

On a road of large semi-detached Edwardian homes, Haydon House distinguishes itself as having the most colorful, pocket-sized garden. Magdalene has made the most of her home, decorating each of the rooms to perfection. Guests enjoy the sitting room with its plump sofas drawn cozily round the fire or the pocket-sized study with just enough room to spread your maps and books to plan the next day's adventures. The bedrooms are exceedingly pretty and named for the color of their decor: Strawberry, Gooseberry, Blueberry, Elderberry, and Mulberry. Request Blueberry or Elderberry if you want a more spacious room. Mulberry, tucked under the eaves, is an especially attractive triple or family room. With a choice of over 80 restaurants in the town, breakfast is the only meal served and includes a fresh-fruit platter and several other alternatives to a traditional, cooked English breakfast. Bath with its graceful, honey-colored buildings, interesting museums, and superb shopping merits several days' exploration. *Directions:* From Bath follow signs onto the A367 towards Radstock and Shepton Mallet. At an elongated roundabout by a railway viaduct, bear left onto Wells Road up a hill to a small shopping area and onto a dual carriageway (The Bear pub is on your right). 300 yards past the shops, fork right into Bloomfield Road and take the second right (by the telephone kiosk) into Bloomfield Park. There is plenty of off-road parking.

HAYDON HOUSE
Owners: Magdalene & Gordon Ashman-Marr
9 Bloomfield Park
Bath
Somerset BA2 2BY, England
Tel & fax: (01225) 444919 & 427351
Email: stay@haydonhouse.co.uk
5 rooms
£35–£49 per person
Open all year, Credit cards: all major
Children welcome, No-smoking house
www.karenbrown.com/england/haydonhouse.html

Bed & Breakfast Descriptions   21

Perched high above the city's rooftops, this large Victorian home offers every comfort to the visitor: luxurious bathrooms with heated towel rails and perfect showers, firm, American queen-sized beds, satellite television, in-house movies, picture-perfect decor, and the sincere attentions of George. Each of the bedrooms has its own flavor and, while I admired those in soft flowery pastels (the pink tower room with its lacy four-poster bed is very popular with honeymooners and there is a spacious ground-floor room for those who have difficulty with stairs), I particularly enjoyed the imaginative four-poster room where four white obelisks are artfully draped in contrasting fabric to form the posts of this most interesting bed. Breakfast in the sunny green and yellow breakfast room offers lots of choices as well as the traditional English cooked breakfast. It's a 15-minute walk into town. George has designed driving tours with detailed instructions for a full day's sightseeing, so guests often venture as far afield as southern Wales. *Directions:* From Bath follows signs onto the A367 towards Exeter, pass an elongated roundabout by a railway viaduct, go up a hill, and take the first turning to the right into Upper Oldfield Park. Holly Lodge is the first house on the right just past the bend.

HOLLY LODGE
Owner: George Hall
8 Upper Oldfield Park
Bath
Somerset BA2 3JZ, England
Tel: (01225) 424042, Fax: (01225) 481138
Email: stay@hollylodge.co.uk
7 rooms
£42–£49 per person
Open all year, Credit cards: all major
Children welcome, No-smoking house
www.karenbrown.com/england/hollylodge.html

Catherine Andrew belongs to that school of dedicated and talented bed and breakfast owners who really take good care of guests with a warm and spontaneous hospitality. She welcomes you to her family home and takes you into her care, brewing you a cup of tea, getting the shortbread, and asking you where you've been and where you're going. Sitting on the sofa in her front room overlooking the garden, it's hard to believe that you are in the midst of a city and not in the countryside. A 15-minute walk finds you in the heart of the city and after a day's sightseeing, you can take a taxi or the bus back up the hill. John arms guests with maps and directions of what to see and where to go. Breakfast is taken at separate little tables in the dining room with a fruit compote and specialties from Catherine's native Scotland on the menu as well as a traditional cooked breakfast. The three bedrooms offer twins, a double, and a queen bed. All are beautifully decorated, with the queen being my especial favorite both for its lovely blue and yellow decor and its wonderful view across the garden and rooftops to Bath and the Royal Crescent. *Directions:* From Bath follow signs onto the A367 towards Radstock and Shepton Mallet. At an elongated roundabout by a railway viaduct, bear left onto Wells Road up a hill to a small shopping area and onto a dual carriageway (The Bear pub is on your right). 300 yards past the shops, fork right into Bloomfield Road and take the second right (by the telephone kiosk) into Bloomfield Park. There is plenty of off-road parking.

MEADOWLAND
Owners: Catherine & John Andrew
36 Bloomfield Park, Bath
Somerset BA2 2BX, England
Tel & fax: (01225) 311079
Email: meadowland@bath92.freeserve.co.uk
3 rooms
£40–£45 per person
Closed Christmas, Credit cards: MC, VS (additional 5%)
Children over 8, No-smoking house
www.karenbrown.com/england/meadowland.html

Situated halfway up a steep hill, Somerset House is a classic Regency abode of warm, honey-colored stone, set in a spacious garden affording panoramic views of the city. The family pets along with family photos and books give a comfortable feeling to the Seymours' upscale guesthouse. Decorated in pastels, the bedrooms have matching drapes and bedspreads and whimsical rag dolls propped up on the pillows. Several rooms have an extra bed and a ground-floor room is ideal for those who have difficulty with stairs. Bedrooms are named after the sons and daughters of George III and in their note to guests Jean and Malcolm have included the child's historical particulars as well as the rules of the house. Innovative buffet, Continental, and English breakfasts are served each morning in the basement dining room with its light-wood Windsor chairs, lace-topped tables, and huge pine dresser set on the checkerboard tile floor. A 12-minute walk brings you into the heart of Bath. *Directions:* Do not go into the city center, but follow signs for the university. Going up Bathwick Hill, Somerset House is on the left.

SOMERSET HOUSE
Owners: Jean, Malcolm & Jonathan Seymour
35 Bathwick Hill
Bath
Somerset BA2 6LD, England
Tel: (01225) 466451, Fax: (01225) 317188
Email: somersethouse@compuserve.com
10 rooms
£32–£36.75 per person
Open all year, Credit cards: all major
Children over 6, No-smoking house
www.karenbrown.com/england/somersethouse.html

Rosamund and John Napier were delighted to find this lovely Georgian House on a quiet street in the conservation village of Bathford just 3 miles from Bath. It was just what they had been looking for—a large home, suitable for bed and breakfast. Over the years they have added bathrooms and showers, decorated, and slowly added antique furniture. It's more comfortably homey than decorator-perfect, with the Napiers' warmth of welcome adding the final ingredient. The spacious sitting room overlooks the grassy garden with its tennis court and guests help themselves to drinks at the honesty bar. Upstairs, the larger bedrooms can be easily adapted to include an extra bed or two for children who just pay for breakfast if sharing their parents' room. Each room is well equipped with color TV, phone, tea-making facilities, hairdryer, and en-suite shower or bathroom. If you would like complete privacy, opt to stay in one of the bedrooms in the walled garden cottage. Bathford is ideally situated for Bath (there are three buses an hour) and within easy reach of Bradford on Avon, Lacock, Longleat House, Stourhead Gardens, Bowood House, and Dyrham Park. *Directions:* From Bath take the A4 towards Chippenham for 3 miles, the A363 towards Bradford on Avon for 100 yards, then turn left up Bathford Hill. Church Street is the first right and Eagle House is on your right after 200 yards.

EAGLE HOUSE
Owners: Rosamund & John Napier
Church Street
Bathford, near Bath
Somerset BA1 7RS, England
Tel: (01225) 859946, Fax: (01225) 859430
Email: jonap@eagleho.demon.co.uk
8 rooms
£32–£38 per person
Closed Christmas & New Year
Credit cards: MC, VS, Children welcome
www.karenbrown.com/england/eaglehouse.html

Formerly an isolated 18th-century woodcutter's cottage, Fox Hole Farm and its cluster of little cottages paint an idyllic pastoral scene. The forest where generations of woodcutters labored is now a reserve ensuring that this will always be a peaceful rural spot. Beamed ceilings and cottage quaintness are the order of the day in the farmhouse where guests have a surprisingly spacious parlor and breakfast room with high-backed chairs drawn invitingly round the log fire and three small tables laid for breakfast. Set just behind the broad chimney breast, the ground-floor bedroom is perfect for those who have difficulty with stairs and offers views of the spot where King Harold camped before the Battle of Hastings. Upstairs, two additional bedrooms are just as cottage-cozy and attractively decorated. All are well equipped with en-suite bathrooms, TVs, and tea-making trays. The cow byre and two barns have been converted into self-catering cottages for two to four persons. Fox Hole Farm's superlative position is just over a mile from Battle, scene of the 1066 Battle of Hastings where William and his invading Normans defeated Harold and his Saxons—you can visit the commemorative embroidery in nearby Hastings. Within easy reach are Rye with its narrow cobbled streets, Winchelsea, Tunbridge Wells, Lewes, and Brighton with its extravagant Royal Pavilion. *Directions:* Leave Battle on the A271 towards Bexhill, take the first right towards Heathfield (B2096), and the entrance to the farm is on your right after ¾ mile.

FOX HOLE FARM
Owners: Pauline & Paul Collins
Kane Hythe Road
Battle
East Sussex TH33 9QU, England
Tel: (01424) 772053, Fax: (01424) 773771
3 rooms, 3 cottages
£24.50–£57 per person, Cottage: £50–£100 per day
Open all year, Credit cards: MC, VS
Children over 10, No-smoking house

Frog Street Farm, a lovely gray-stone farmhouse dating back to 1436, is a real working farm where things are not fancy or cutesy-pretty, but everything fits together perfectly with country freshness. From the moment you are met at the door by Veronica, with her true country-style warmth and jolly sense of humor, the mood is set. You are immediately made to feel part of the family and offered a cup of tea in front of the large inglenook fireplace before being shown to your room. The guestrooms are spotlessly clean and simply but prettily decorated throughout with a color scheme of pinks and greens. Behind the house lies the farmyard, while to the front is a colorful garden. Veronica takes great pride in her cooking and, with advance notice, will prepare delicious meals from farm-fresh produce. For those who want to spend a few days in the country, away from city sophistication, Frog Street Farm is the epitome of what a farm vacation should be. In this pretty, rolling countryside are the charming little towns of Chard, Ilchester, Ilminster, and Crewkerne. To the north the limestone Mendip Hills are honeycombed with spectacular caves and gorges such as Wookey Hole and Cheddar Gorge. The magnificent cathedral city of Wells is within easy driving distance. *Directions:* From the M5 take exit 25 and continue 4½ miles southeast to Hatch Beauchamp. Take Station Road to Frog Street Farm.

FROG STREET FARM
Owners: Veronica & Henry Cole
Beercrocombe
Taunton
Somerset TA3 6AF, England
Tel & fax: (01823) 480430
3 rooms
£25–£30 per person, dinner £10–£16
Open Apr to Oct, Credit cards: none
Children over 11, No-smoking house
www.karenbrown.com/england/frogstreet.html

Set in a luxuriant garden, this 14th-century thatched Dartmoor longhouse, one of only a handful remaining, presents an idyllic picture. Guests are welcomed with tea on the lawn in summer and immediately made to feel at home. The house has lots of charming features such as enormous granite fireplaces, sloping walls, low doors, exposed beams, and low, often sloping ceilings. The three small double bedrooms at the top of the steep, narrow staircase are cottage-cozy, each with a double four-poster bed, which hugs the ceiling. Two bedrooms have snug en-suite shower rooms while the third has its shower across the hall. There are many old, characterful pubs and restaurants nearby for dinner. Tor Down House is in Dartmoor National Park and a short walk up the lane finds you amidst the bracken and climbing up to the rugged tors. Gardens are popular with visitors and in the next village is one featuring the national collection of hostas. Rosemoor, the Royal Horticultural Society garden, is also nearby. This is an ideal base offering easy access to the West Country. *Directions:* Leave the A30 at the junction signposted Okehampton and Belstone (there are two Okehampton junctions). Follow signs for Belstone (2 miles) and in the center of the village take the lane that turns right immediately after the post office. You find Tor Down House's wooden five-bar gate after ¾ mile, soon after crossing the cattle grid.

TOR DOWN HOUSE
Owners: Maureen & John Pakenham
Belstone, Okehampton
Devon EX20 1QY, England
Tel & fax: (01837) 840731
Email: info@tordownhouse.co.uk
3 rooms
£35 per person
Closed Christmas & New Year, Credit cards: MC, VS
Children over 14, No-smoking house
www.karenbrown.com/england/tordown.html

Set in 2 private acres high on a hill overlooking the River Tweed and with views towards Berwick-upon-Tweed, the coast, and the distant Cheviot Hills, High Letham is a fully restored Georgian farmhouse, dating back over 200 years. Hosts Richard and Susan Persse provide guests with three comfortable bedrooms, a double with private bathroom en suite and two twins, each with its own en-suite shower room. A log fire crackles in the sitting room overlooking the walled garden. Susan's cooking is complemented by wines from the house list put together by Richard, drawing on skills from his previous life as a wine merchant. The Old Barn, adjacent to the farmhouse proper, fully appointed for self-catering and sleeping six, has one double-bedded room and two twin-bedded rooms sharing two bathrooms. Fishing abounds in the area and can be arranged locally. There are fine walks along the Tudor fortifications encircling Berwick and you can visit the castles and historic towns of the borders. Drive over the causeway at low tide to Holy Island to see the ruins of the abbey where monks illuminated the Lindisfarne Gospels over 13 centuries ago. The island is presided over by snug Lindesfarne Castle, built in Tudor times and remodeled in 1903 by Lutyens. *Directions:* From the south take the A1 around Berwick, cross the river, take the first left, and turn immediately right up a narrow lane. At the top of the hill turn left and High Letham Farmhouse is on your left.

HIGH LETHAM FARMHOUSE   **New**
Owners: Susan & Richard Persse
By Berwick-upon-Tweed
Northumberland TD15 1UX, England
Tel: (01289) 306585, Fax: (01289) 304194
Email: hlfk@fantasyprints.co.uk
3 rooms, 1 cottage
£30–£34 per person, dinner £22
Cottage £190–£415 per week
Closed Christmas, Credit cards: MC, VS
Children over 12, No-smoking house
www.karenbrown.com/england/highletham.html

Middle Ord Manor is the most spacious of homes, built over 200 years ago as the landowner's residence for the Grey family. There have always been Greys here, though Geoffrey and Joan are not relations. They are the first to spell their name with an "a" and the first to farm the estate rather than supervise it. Joan has a welcoming way with guests and has packed a table in the spacious upstairs sitting room with enough information on things to do to keep you busy for a fortnight. The spacious bedrooms are kitted out with every extra, from a trouser press to homemade biscuits. The beds—a double four-poster, twins, and a king—are comfortable and each room has its own shower room. For those who wish to take a bath, there is an additional bathroom. Breakfast is the only meal served but Joan has all the menus of local eateries on hand so that guests can choose one that fits their fancy. Nearby Berwick is a historic town within two sets of walls. You reach nearby Lindisfarne (Holy Island) by a causeway from the mainland at low tide and Joan has a tide table showing the safe crossing times. Lindisfarne mead is made there and the factory is open to the public. Bamburgh, Alnwick, and Floors Castles are all close at hand. *Directions:* Remain on the A1 bypass around Berwick-upon-Tweed and take the A698 towards Cornhill for ¼ mile. At the small fingerpost sign on your right, turn left for Middle Ord and follow the lane to the house.

MIDDLE ORD MANOR
Owners: Joan & Geoffrey Gray
Middle Ord
Berwick-upon-Tweed
Northumberland TD15 2XQ, England
Tel: (01289) 306323, Fax: (01289) 308423
Email: joangray@middleordmanor.co.uk
3 rooms
£29 per person
Open Easter to Oct, Credit cards: none
Children over 16, No-smoking house
www.karenbrown.com/england/middleord.html

Kath and Tony Peacock live in what was Boltongate's large, rambling rectory, which dates from 1360 but was extensively "modernized" in Victorian times. Many of its rooms face south and have delightful views of peaceful countryside with distant views of the Lakeland fells and mountains. In summer the sun streams in and guests can enjoy the garden with its ponds and arbors, while during the cooler months log fires burn in the study and dining room. Dining in the cozy oak-beamed dining room is a delightful experience. In contrast to the old-world dining room, the bedrooms and sitting room are spacious, tall-ceilinged, large-windowed rooms. Bedrooms are large and comfortable, decorated with pretty wallpapers and matching drapes. Two have en-suite bathrooms while the largest has its bathroom (robes provided) down the hall. Boltongate is on the quiet, northernmost fringes of the Lake District, a perfect spot to break a journey to or from Scotland. Pretty towns and villages such as Caldbeck, Borrowdale, Ullswater, and Buttermere abound. William Wordsworth's birthplace is nearby in Cockermouth. *Directions:* From the Keswick bypass take the A591 for 7 miles. At the Castle Inn turn right at the sign for Ireby. Drive through Ireby to Boltongate (1½ miles). The Rectory is the first house on the right as you come up the hill.

BOLTONGATE OLD RECTORY
Owners: Kathleen & Anthony Peacock
Boltongate
Cumbria CA5 1DA, England
Tel: (016973) 71647, Fax: (016973) 71798
Email: boltongate@aol.com
3 rooms
£38–£40 per person, dinner £19.50
Closed Christmas & New Year, Credit cards: MC, VS
Children over 14, No-smoking house
www.karenbrown.com/england/boltongateoldrectory.html

"Everything's coming up roses" at Cawthorpe Hall—acres and acres of them perfume the air from May to September at this rose farm where Chantal and Ozric Armstrong produce rose oil and rose water. Guests who stay at harvest time are welcome to join dawn picking forays and to help with the distillation of the fragrant blooms. Like its roses, Cawthorpe Hall is a delightfully rambling place with various additions since 1819 when the main house was built. One addition was a light-filled artist's studio, which today serves as the guests' sitting and dining room and a gallery for daughter Dominique's paintings. It's a very interesting room with wicker chairs from Chantal's native Madeira round the breakfast table, an antique dresser adorned with African artifacts collected when the family lived abroad, and comfortable armchairs drawn close to the wood-burning stove. My favorite of the three bedrooms is the spacious ground-floor queen-bedded room with its tall bay windows framing a garden view and its seating area beside the wood-burning stove. Breakfast is the only meal served so for dinner guests usually go to The Wishing Well in the adjacent hamlet of Dyke. Many guests visit Burghley House, Belton House, Belvoir Castle, and Stamford where *Middlemarch* was filmed. *Directions:* Exit the A1 at Stamford, take the A6121 to Bourne, then the A15 towards Sleaford. Leave Bourne and take the first left turn into the hamlet of Cawthorpe. Cawthorpe Hall is the last house on the right where the road turns into a track.

CAWTHORPE HALL
Owners: Chantal & Ozric Armstrong
Cawthorpe
Bourne, Lincolnshire PE10 0AB, England
Tel: (01778) 423830, Fax: (01778) 426620
Email: bandb@rosewater.co.uk
3 rooms
£30 per person
Closed Christmas & New Year, Credit cards: none
Children welcome, No-smoking house
www.karenbrown.com/england/cawthorpe.html

Wooded slopes and hills fold down to the vast expanse of Lake Windermere where Bowness began life as a little lakeside village. Now it's a tourist center with water skiing, a yacht club, and ferries that ply the lake. Just a four-minute walk from the hubbub you find Low Fell, a lovely turn-of-the-century house sheltered behind a high wall in an acre of landscaped gardens, the friendly, welcoming home of Louise and Stephen Broughton, and their daughters. The Broughtons have lots of experience in where to go and what to see as they own a mini-coach touring company, The Mountain Goat. You can opt for one of their day trips or, if you prefer, Louise or Stephen will sit with you in the guests' sitting-cum-breakfast room and help you plan your sightseeing. I especially liked the skylit attic suite (lots of narrow stairs) with its comfy beds topped with goose-down comforters in the twin and double bedrooms, bathroom, and kitchen with fridge. An additional king-bedded/twin-bedded room with en-suite shower room overlooks the garden. Louise serves a scrumptious breakfast—be sure to try her pancakes! There are some excellent little restaurants and pubs in the village for dinner. Within a 20-minute drive are Dove Cottage, Rydal Mount, and the villages of Ambleside and Grasmere. Take the car ferry across the lake to visit Beatrix Potter's Hill Top Farm in Near Sawrey. *Directions:* From Windermere follow signs to the lake and Bowness. Bear left at Barclays Bank and first left opposite the church. Follow the road past two hotels and a small garage on the left—Low Fell is the large cream house on your right.

LOW FELL COUNTRY HOUSE
Owners: Louise & Stephen Broughton
Ferney Green, Bowness on Windermere
Cumbria LA23 3ES, England
Tel: (015394) 45612, Fax: (015394) 48411
Email: lowfell@talk21.com
3 rooms
£25–£30 per person
Closed Christmas & New Year, Credit cards: MC, VS
Children welcome, No-smoking house
www.karenbrown.com/england/lowfell.html

Priory Steps, a row of 17th-century weavers' cottages high above the town of Bradford on Avon, is a glorious place to stay. The village tumbles down the hill to the banks of the River Avon, its narrow streets full of interesting shops and antique dealers. A few miles distant, the glories of Bath await exploration and are easily accessible by car or the local train service. Hostess Diana is a gourmet cook and guests dine *en famille* in the traditionally furnished dining room. While Diana's cooking is reason enough to spend several days here, the adjacent library with its books and pamphlets highlighting the many places to visit in the area provides additional justification. The bedrooms are all very different, each accented with antique furniture, and each has a smart modern bathroom, television, and tea and coffee tray. The Blue Room has large shuttered and curtained windows and a pleasing decor in shades of blue and pink, while the large English Room has striped paper in muted tones of green coordinating with flowered curtains. There is a touch of whimsy in the bathroom of the dark-beamed Frog Room where an odd frog or two has inspired former guests to send their own contributions to an ever-growing collection of the creatures. The frogless bedroom itself is very pretty. *Directions:* Take the A363 from Bath to Bradford on Avon. As the road drops steeply into the town, Newtown is the first road to the right. Priory Steps is 150 yards on the left.

PRIORY STEPS
Owners: Diana & Carey Chapman
Newtown
Bradford on Avon
Wiltshire BA15 1NQ, England
Tel: (01225) 862230, Fax: (01225) 866248
Email: priorysteps@clara.co.uk
5 rooms
£37–£42 per person, dinner £22
Open all year, Credit cards: MC, VS
Children over 12
www.karenbrown.com/england/priorysteps.html

When Brafferton-Helperby, with its Viking origins, was a bustling river port it had 13 busy pubs but now it's a quiet little village just off the A1 midway between London and Edinburgh, and within easy driving distance of York. Just a three-minute walk from the heart of the village, Laurel Manor Farm, a tall, classic Georgian home, sits overlooking the Vale of York. Annie and Sam offer a sincerely warm welcome to their home where Annie ensures that you are well taken care of and Sam takes the time to discuss with you where to go and what to see—he has a map of over 200 things to see and do within an hour's drive. Relax in the evening in the very comfortable drawing room and enjoy breakfast in the dining room round the circular oak gate-leg table. For dinner there is no shortage of nearby restaurants and country pubs. The three bedrooms are named after the three "ridings" that used to make up the county of Yorkshire. North Riding is a prettily papered suite with a double-bedded room, single room, and an en-suite bathroom. East Riding is a delightful twin-bedded room with a snug en-suite shower room. West Riding sports a four-poster bed and has its private bathroom across the hall. Annie raises horses and is often found working in her award-winning garden. Laurel Manor Farm is ideal for exploring the Yorkshire Dales and Moors, Castle Howard, Whitby, and York. *Directions:* Leave the A1 at Boroughbridge and follow the Easingwold road to Helperby. Turn right at the junction and right again up Hall Lane: Laurel Manor Farm is on your left after 100 yards.

LAUREL MANOR FARM
Owners: Annie & Sam Key
Brafferton-Helperby
North Yorkshire YO61 2NZ, England
Tel: (01423) 360436, Fax: (01423) 360437
Email: laurelmf@aol.com
3 rooms
£30–£35 per person
Open all year, Credit cards: none
Children welcome
www.karenbrown.com/england/laurel.html

Barbara and Barrie found the perfect home in this gracious Georgian house in Brampford Speke, a delightful little village just outside Exeter. Guests use the large drawing room, which opens up to the spacious conservatory where they often join Barbara and Barrie for a drink in the evening. Barbara serves a delicious breakfast in the dining room with lots of choices of fruit and cereal on the buffet along with cheese and ham and strawberry crepes in addition to the traditional cooked breakfast. Upstairs are two very attractive bedrooms, each accompanied by a dressing room and large bathroom. An additional smaller twin bedroom may be combined with the larger one to make a private suite. Barbara really makes an effort to help you plan day trips, lending maps and booklets, and directing you to nearby spots featured in Jane Austen's *Sense and Sensibility*. From here you can visit the north and south Devon coasts while closer at hand is Dartmoor. It's an ideal place to stay if you are attending the Exeter music festival, which takes place for three weeks in July. For dinner, guests often walk to the nearby Agricultural Inn, which serves good pub food as well as having a restaurant, and Barbara has a list of recommended pubs farther afield. *Directions:* From Exeter take the A377 towards Crediton. After passing over the Exe bridge on the outskirts of town, turn right to Brampford Speke and Brampford House is on the left in the village, just beyond the church and before the red telephone box.

BRAMPFORD HOUSE
Owners: Barbara & Barrie Smith
Brampford Speke, near Exeter
Devon EX 5 5DW, England
Tel: (01392) 841195, Fax (01392) 841196
3 rooms
£22–£35 per person
Open Mar to Oct, Credit cards: none
Children over 8, No-smoking house
www.karenbrown.com/england/brampfordhouse.html

Gently rolling hills with sheep grazing peacefully and shaded valleys with meandering streams surround the picturesque village of Broad Campden where The Malt House hugs the quiet main street and opens up at the rear to a beautiful garden. Years ago barley was made into malt here for brewing beer. Now a picturesque, country house, it provides a perfect central location for exploring other Cotswold villages. It is very much a family operation with Nick and Jean at the front of the house and son Julian as the talented chef. Julian offers three choices for each of the three dinner courses served in the inviting dining room where an open fire blazes on chilly evenings. Of the two lounges the little sitting room with its comfortable chairs arranged round the massive inglenook fireplace and mullioned windows offering glimpses of the garden is a favorite place to relax and toast your toes by the fire in winter. The bedroom decor ranges from cottage-cozy to contemporary, and most of the immaculate bathrooms have old-fashioned tubs. Five bedrooms are in the house while an inviting ground-floor suite and two bedrooms are in the stable block. Lovely Cotswold villages to explore include Chipping Campden, Bourton-on-the-Water, Upper and Lower Slaughter, Stow-on-the-Wold, Bibury, and Broadway. Garden lovers will enjoy Kiftsgate, Hidcote Manor, and Batsford. *Directions:* On entering Chipping Campden, take the first right: you know you are in Broad Campden when you see the Bakers Arms. The Malt House is opposite the wall topped by a tall topiary hedge.

THE MALT HOUSE
Owners: Jean, Julian & Nick Brown
Broad Campden, Chipping Campden
Gloucestershire GL55 6UU, England
Tel: (01386) 840295, Fax: (01386) 841334
Email: nick@the-malt-house.freeserve.co.uk
8 rooms
£47.25–£58.50 per person, dinner £29.50 (not Tues or Wed)
Closed Christmas, Credit cards: all major
Children over 5
www.karenbrown.com/england/themalthouse.html

Barn House is the most handsome, stone 17th-century house set on Broadway's High Street in 16 acres of paddocks and gardens, which are open to the public (monies collected are donated to a local charity). Overnight guests are privileged to enjoy this peaceful setting and lovely house with its beautiful gardens and outdoor, enclosed swimming pool. In the evening you can relax in the Great Hall, an awesome sitting room with soaring ceilings and blackened beams or in the smaller, cozier sitting room. Four spacious guestrooms are found down long, narrow hallways whose floors are covered with tapestry runners. The rooms are set behind high pine doors with brass knockers. A twin room features a picture of Mark and friend jumping in an equestrian competition; a large double room enjoys a sitting area, enormous bath, and old, exposed, pine beams; the Pink Room with a king bed and sitting area can be shared with a small double that overlooks the courtyard garden. The Garden Suite enjoys a large sitting area with TV, a bedroom with a double bed, a small kitchen, and windows looking out across the croquet lawn to sheep pature beyond. Breakfast is served in the delightful dining room. *Directions:* Broadway is off the A44 between Evesham and Stow-on-the-Wold. Drive through town on High Street with the Lygon Arms on the left, and Barn House is just a few blocks farther, past the shops on the same side of the street.

BARN HOUSE
Owners: Jane & Mark Ricketts
152 High Street
Broadway
Worcestershire WR12 7AJ, England
Tel & fax: (01386) 858633
Email: barnhouse@btinternet.com
4 rooms
£25–£35 per person
Open all year, Credit cards: none
Children welcome
www.karenbrown.com/england/barnhouse.html

A handsome gold-on-blue sign advertising bed and breakfast accommodation caught our attention soon after we left Broadway and tempted us down a country lane. The next sign, "Drive Slowly—Free Range Children and Animals" made us chuckle, so we stopped to look around. With Sue Adams looking for something to occupy her time now that her children require less attention, her husband, Mike, converted the central section of their home to accommodate overnight guests. Three comfortably sized guestrooms are fresh in their newness and pretty in their decor of light-pine furniture against cream walls. Two rooms are found on either side of the entry and the third is tucked under the angled roofline. While guests do not have a sitting room, they sometimes settle in the evening at the tables in the breakfast room where a library of books is available to browse through and views look out to the surrounding greenery. The Adams ask that guests not use the deck directly behind the home as this is established as their private family area, but guests can relax on the front flagstone terrace. At the edge of the property trails lead down to the fields and along the Cotswold Way. *Directions:* Travel the A44 east from Broadway and just before the intersection for Chipping Campden, look for their sign on the right stating "Country House B&B."

HIGHLANDS COUNTRY HOUSE
Owners: Susan & Mike Adams
Fish Hill
Broadway
Worcestershire WR12 7LD, England
Tel: (01386) 858015, Fax: (01386) 852584
3 rooms
£27.50 per person
Closed Dec, Credit cards: none
Children welcome, No-smoking house

Broadway with its attractive shops is one of the loveliest Cotswold villages and certainly one of the busiest. A stay at Milestone House not only gives you the opportunity to enjoy the village after the daytime crowds have left but also provides a convenient base for exploring this lovely part of the country. Like many of the houses in the village, Milestone House was built in the early part of the 17th century and is full of period charm. Guests have two comfortable sitting rooms and a large sunny conservatory where breakfast is served overlooking the garden. At dinner time guests choose from the array of eating establishments in Broadway and the surrounding villages. Up the narrow staircase you find three comfortable bedrooms. The two at the front of the house have shower rooms while a third enjoys a larger bathroom and overlooks the garden. Guests who are staying longer than a couple of nights particularly enjoy the courtyard room with its own private entrance. Helen and Gerald take lots of interest in their guests and assist in planning their itineraries, with information on off-the-beaten-track Cotswold villages. *Directions:* Broadway is off the A44 between Evesham and Stow-on-the-Wold. Milestone House is located on the Upper High Street with a car park to the rear.

MILESTONE HOUSE
Owners: Helen & Gerald Norman
122 Upper High Street
Broadway
Worcestershire WR12 7AJ, England
Tel & fax: (01386) 853432
Email: milestone.house@talk21.com
4 rooms
£27.50–£32.50 per person
Open all year, Credit cards: MC, VS
Children welcome, No-smoking house
www.karenbrown.com/england/milestonehouse.html

Just a five-minute walk from the center of bustling Broadway and you are on a quiet country lane that leads to Top Farm. Converted from a 200-year-old barn over 20 years ago, this is now the spacious home of Doreen and Granville Shaw and their golden retriever Bertie who never fails to offer a tail-wagging welcome. Doreen ran a larger bed and breakfast in town for several years, moving to Top Farm in 1999 to scale down and enjoy her large garden and the spaciousness of her home. The guest sitting room is in the former barn with its high, raftered ceiling and enough room for a sitting area with TV below and a loft large enough to house a pool table. Breakfast is the only meal served in the dining room and for dinner guests often walk down to Oliver's Wine Bar or enjoy pub food at The Crown and Trumpet. Both of the bedrooms (one a twin and one a double) are paneled in old pine and have their own en-suite bathrooms. There is no shortage of things to do hereabouts as Broadway is very central for exploring lovely mellow-stone Cotswold villages and famous gardens. A delightful day trip takes you farther afield to Stratford-upon-Avon and Warwick Castle. *Directions:* Broadway is off the A44 between Evesham and Stow-on-the-Wold. Drive through town on High Street with the Lygon Arms on the left and as the road goes up the hill look for Bibsworth Lane to the left. Top Farm is the last house on the right with open garages across the lane.

TOP FARM
Owners: Doreen & Granville Shaw
Bibsworth Lane
Broadway
Worcestershire WR12 7LW, England
Tel & fax: (01386) 853375
2 rooms
£25 per person
Closed Christmas, Credit cards: none
Children over 16, No-smoking house

The taste of Augill Castle is truly delicious. It is the most imposing home—a flamboyant Victorian castle built by a local eccentric who used to greet his guests regally from a dais in the hallway. No regality to Wendy and Simon's warm welcome! They have rescued this impressive place from abandonment and returned it to its former glory, adding spacious bathrooms to the bedrooms, furnishing with antiques, and redecorating with their own hands the whole of this vast house. You will see what a task that has been when you look at the "before" picture in every room. Toast your toes by the fire in the magnificent music room and dine with your fellow guests round the 12-foot-long dining table in the blue Gothic dining hall. Wendy and Simon offer a set four-course dinner, tailoring it to guests' likes and dislikes. The meat is organic and comes from a nearby hillfarm. The bedrooms are stunning and several are positively palatial—discuss your preferences when you book: magnificent four-poster bed, soaking tub for two, oak paneling, a walk-in turret, Gothic leaded windows are just some of the choices. Sitting in the Eden Valley between the Yorkshire Dales and the Lake District, Augill Castle is an ideal several-day stopover on your way south or north. *Directions:* Exit the M6 at junction 38 and take the A685 through Kirkby Stephen towards Brough-in-Westmorland. Go through Brough Sowerby and turn right at the signpost for South Stainmore. The castle is on your left after 1 mile.

AUGILL CASTLE
Owners: Wendy & Simon Bennett
Brough-in-Westmorland, Kirkby Stephen
Cumbria CA17 4DE, England
Tel: (017683) 41937, Fax: (017683) 41936
Email: augill@aol.com
6 rooms
£40–£50 per person, dinner £22.50
Open all year, Credit cards: MC, VS
Children welcome, No-smoking house
www.karenbrown.com/england/augill.html

Dorset is synonymous with Thomas Hardy for it is here amongst these lovely villages that he was born and set his novels. An ideal base for explorations is Holyleas House, a welcoming house in apple-pie order and home to Tia and Julian Bunkall. After a day exploring, make yourself at home in the guests' sitting room—toast your toes by the log fire and browse the selection of interesting books. Enjoy breakfast round the long polished dining-room table—eggs come from the hens roaming the garden, jams are homemade, and there's a vegetarian alternative to the traditional cooked breakfast. The premier bedroom is the spacious twin/king with its views both to the village lane and the garden and a snug en-suite shower room. A double-bedded room has a bath with shower overlooking the garden while a single-bedded room has its private bathroom up the hallway. As well as visiting Hardy's home and the setting of his books, from here you can easily explore several interesting towns and villages: Milton Abbas, an 18th-century show village of white and golden thatched cottages; Cerne Abbas with its thatched Tudor cottages overlooked by a 180-ft giant carved into the hillside; Sherborne, an architectural feast of golden-stone buildings and a castle built by Sir Walter Raleigh; and Dorchester, the Casterbridge of Hardy's novels. *Directions:* From Dorchester take the A35 towards Poole for a short way to the B3143 through Piddlehinton and Piddletrentide to Buckland Newton. Holyleas House is on the right just over the crossroads opposite the village cricket pitch.

HOLYLEAS HOUSE
Owners: Tia & Julian Bunkall
Buckland Newton
Dorset DT2 7DP, England
Tel: (01300) 345214, Fax: (01305) 264488
Email: tiabunkall@holyleas.fsnet.co.uk
3 rooms
£25–£27 per person
Closed Christmas, Credit cards: none
Children welcome, No-smoking house
www.karenbrown.com/england/holyleas.html

New House Farm sits beside the lane surrounded by green fields beneath rugged Lakeland peaks. Hazel grew up at a hotel and returned here with her young children to provide gracious guest accommodation in this 17th-century farmhouse and transform the barn into a tea room and restaurant. Flagstone floors, beamed ceilings, and old fireplaces are the order of the day in the farmhouse. Hazel prepares a set, five-course dinner, but if you prefer a lighter, less formal meal, walk across to the barn where little tables and chairs are arranged in the old cow stalls, specials are posted on the board, and main courses include quiche, fish, and steak. Upstairs, two of the country-cozy bedrooms offer zip-link beds and en-suite bathrooms while the other two are snug double-bedded rooms with en-suite shower rooms. My favorite room lies a few steps from the house in the former stables—its ground-floor location makes it ideal for those who have difficulty with stairs. New House Farm sits amid the rugged scenery that has made the Lake District such a draw for centuries. Stride up Grasmoor or follow the country lane to Crummock Water and Buttermere from where the road winds and twists over the fells to Rosthwaite, Grange, and Keswick. *Directions:* From exit 40 on the M6 take the A66 past Keswick, and turn left onto the B5292 to Lorton. Follow signs for Buttermere on the B5289 south and New House Farm is on your left after 2 miles.

NEW HOUSE FARM
Owner: Hazel Thompson
Buttermere Valley
Cumbria CA13 9UU, England
Tel & fax: (01900) 85404
Email: hazel@newhousefarm.co.uk
5 rooms
£40–£44 per person, dinner £22
Open all year, Credit cards: MC, VS
Children over 6, No-smoking house
www.karenbrown.com/england/newhousefarm.html

The Old Rectory was once the palace of the Bishop of Thetford, whose main duty was to "stand by" in case the Bishop of Norwich needed him to "stand in." The wise bishop built himself this lovely home in a picturesque spot convenient for stand-in duty, which means that guests here can enjoy countryside peace and quiet while having Norwich on their doorstep and easy access to the Broads and quaint Suffolk villages. This delectable home is surrounded by lovely gardens and paddocks of grazing horses and its interior is just as appealing, with beautifully decorated rooms furnished with enviable antiques and old paintings. The double-bedded guestroom enjoys views to the front and side of the house and has an en-suite bathroom. An equally lovely twin-bedded room has its bathroom across the hall. An additional single-bedded room is available in conjunction with either of the other rooms. Kassy and Jonathan make themselves very available to guests and you will doubtless meet their two friendly lurchers and family cat. Nearby Norwich is rich in historic treasures including a beautiful Norman cathedral and a castle built by one of William the Conqueror's supporters (now the Castle Museum). The popular Norfolk Broads are full of bird life and boating enthusiasts. *Directions:* From Norwich, take the A140 signposted for Ipswich for 1 mile to the big roundabout at the junction of the A47 and A140. Take the minor road signposted to Caistor St. Edmund. After 1 mile turn left at the crossroads and The Old Rectory is immediately on your right.

THE OLD RECTORY
Owners: Kassy & Jonathan Pusey
Caistor St. Edmund, Norwich
Norfolk NR14 8QS, England
Tel: (01508) 492490, Fax: (01508) 495172
3 rooms
£30 per person
Closed occasionally, Credit cards: MC, VS
Children over 8, No-smoking house

Built over a century ago, Chilvester Hill House is a solidly constructed Victorian home isolated from the busy A4 by a large garden. Gill and John Dilley retired here and subsequently unretired themselves: John, a physician, now works as an occupational health consultant and Gill entertains guests and breeds beef cattle. Gill enjoys cooking and a typical (optional) dinner might consist of smoked trout, lamb noisettes with vegetables from the garden, fruit fool, and cheese and biscuits. They have a short wine list with over 20 French and German wines. A soft pastel decor, treasured antiques, and a cleverly displayed collection of commemorative plates make the large, high-ceilinged drawing room the most elegant room in the house. The bedrooms are spacious, high-ceilinged rooms, each individually decorated with flowery wallpaper and two have zip-link beds that can be either a king or twins. All have mineral water, tea and coffee tray, television, tourist information, and private bathroom. Visitors can take advantage of Gill and John's maps marked with scenic routes to nearby Castle Combe, Lacock, and the Avebury Neolithic Circle. Bath, Oxford, and Salisbury are an easy drive away. *Directions:* From London leave the M4 at junction 14 and follow signs for Hungerford. Turn right on the A4 through Marlborough to Calne. Follow Chippenham signs for half a mile, turn right (Bremhill), and immediately right into the drive.

CHILVESTER HILL HOUSE
Owners: Gill & John Dilley
Calne
Wiltshire SN11 0LP, England
Tel: (01249) 813981, Fax: (01249) 814217
Email: gill.dilley@talk21.com
3 rooms
£37.50–£42.50 per person, dinner £18–£25
Open all year, Credit cards: all major
Children over 12
www.karenbrown.com/england/chilvester.html

Magnolia House, a sturdy Georgian home converted into the most welcoming of guest houses by Ann and John Davies, sits on a quiet street just a five-minute walk from the heart of Canterbury. Ann and John offer a sincerely warm welcome to their home and mark up maps of the city so that guests can easily find their way around. A small parlor is stacked with information not only on Canterbury but the surrounding area—you can easily keep busy for a week. Delightful guestrooms are found upstairs in the house ranging in size from a snug single to lovely double-bedded room, but the gem is the Garden Room with its private garden entrance, four-poster queen-sized bed, and the most spacious of bathrooms. In summer breakfast is the only meal served but on gloomy winter evenings Ann realizes that very often guests do not want to venture out and is happy, with prior arrangement, to provide supper. Canterbury is a lively historical city easily explored on foot. Its primary attraction is its cathedral, the Mother Church for all Anglicans. Begun in 1070, it has survived fires, wars, desecration, and bombing and became a pilgrimage site after the murder of Thomas à Becket. Join Chaucer's famous pilgrims in a 20th-century re-enactment of the *Canterbury Tales* at the Canterbury Tales Museum in St. Margaret's Street. *Directions:* Arriving in Canterbury on the A2, at the first roundabout turn left for the university. St. Dunstan's Terrace is the third street on the right and Magnolia House is the first house on the left.

MAGNOLIA HOUSE
Owners: Ann & John Davies
36 St. Dunstan's Terrace
Canterbury CT2 8AX, England
Tel & fax: (01227) 765121
Email: magnolia_house_canterbury@yahoo.com
7 rooms
£43–£63 per person, dinner (Nov to Feb) from £23
Open all year, Credit cards: all major
Children over 12, No-smoking house
www.karenbrown.com/england/magnolia.html

Because of its quiet country location just 3 miles off the motorway, almost equidistant between Edinburgh and London, New Capernwray Farm is an ideal place to break a long, tiring journey. However, many weary travelers return for a proper country getaway to explore this unspoiled area. There really is nothing "new" about this solid, whitewashed stone farmhouse, for, despite its name, it is over 300 years old. It was bought in 1974 by Sally and Peter Townend, who supervised its complete refurbishment while preserving its lovely old features, and now offer a very warm welcome to their guests. Before dinner you enjoy an aperitif in the cozy sitting room in front of a cheerful fire and then proceed to the dining room for a candlelit dinner. Bedrooms are particularly light, bright, and cheerful in their decor. The largest bedroom, with king bed, spans the breadth of the house, has a bathroom tucked neatly under the eaves and, as in all the rooms, is well equipped with tea, coffee, biscuits, television, hairdryer, mints, and a substantial sewing kit. A twin-bedded room has an en-suite shower room and the queen-bedded room has its shower room nearby. Sally and Peter have a wealth of books and maps on the Lake District and the Yorkshire Dales. *Directions:* Leave the M6 at junction 35 and from the roundabout follow signs for Over Kellet. Turn left at the T-junction into Over Kellet, then turn left at the village green: after 2 miles the farm is on the left.

NEW CAPERNWRAY FARM
Owners: Sally & Peter Townend
Capernwray, Carnforth
Lancashire LA6 1AD, England
Tel & fax: (01524) 734284
Email: newcapfarm@aol.com
3 rooms
£33–£39 per person, dinner £19.50
Open Mar to Oct, Credit cards: MC, VS
Children over 10, No-smoking house
www.karenbrown.com/england/newcapernwrayfarm.html

Carlisle makes an excellent place to break the journey when driving between England and Scotland. Your host, Philip Parker, an ardent enthusiast of Carlisle and the surrounding area, encourages guests to use Number Thirty One as a base for visiting the city and exploring the northern Lake District and Hadrian's Wall. One of Philip's great passions is cooking and the dinner he prepares for guests depends on what is fresh in the market that day. Philip and Judith often join guests for a chat after dinner. Upstairs, the three bedrooms are equipped to a very high standard, with TV, trouser press, tea tray, and hairdryer, and furnished in a style complementing this large Victorian terrace home. I admired the spaciousness of the Blue Room with its sparkling Mediterranean bathroom and king-sized bed and enjoyed the sunny decor of the smaller Green Room with its large golden dragon stenciled on the black headboard. The equally attractive Yellow Room has a half-tester bed that can be king-sized or twin and faces the front of the house. A ten-minute stroll finds you in the heart of Carlisle with its majestic cathedral, grand castle, and Tullie House museum, which portrays Carlisle's place in the turbulent history of the Borders. In 1999 Philip and Judith were awarded the prestigious "B&B of the Year" by England for Excellence. *Directions:* Leave the M6 at junction 43 and follow Carlisle City Centre signs through five sets of traffic lights (the fifth is for pedestrians). Howard Place is the next turning on the right (before you reach the one-way system). Number 31 is at the end of the street on the left.

NUMBER THIRTY ONE
Owners: Judith & Philip Parker
31 Howard Place
Carlisle, Cumbria CA1 1HR, England
Tel & fax: (01228) 597080
Email: bestpep@aol.com
3 rooms
£40–£47.50 per person, dinner from £25
Open Mar to Nov, Credit cards: all major
Children over 16, No-smoking house
www.karenbrown.com/england/numberthirtyone.html

Teresa White, who hails from Edinburgh, prides herself on offering a warm Scottish welcome to her up-market bed-and-breakfast hotel located a brisk 20-minute walk from the heart of medieval Chester. When she bought Redland in the 1980s, it was very different from the flower-decked, frothily Victorian establishment you find today. Teresa has kept all the lovely woodwork and ornate plasterwork, adding modern bathrooms, central heating, vast quantities of sturdy Victorian furniture, four suits of armor, and masses of Victorian bric-a-brac. Guests help themselves to drinks at the honesty bar and relax in the sumptuous drawing room, which includes among its array of furniture high-backed armchairs that almost surround you. Traditional Scottish porridge is a must when you order breakfast in the dining room where little tables are covered with starched Victorian tablecloths. For dinner Teresa is happy to advise on where to eat in town. Pay the few extra pounds and request one of the "best" rooms, for not only are they more spacious, but you will be treated to a lovely old bed (with modern mattress, of course) and decor where everything from the draperies to the china is color-coordinated. Walking round Chester's Roman walls is a good way to orient yourself to the city. It is fun to browse in The Rows, double-decker layers of shops. *Directions:* Redland Hotel is located on the A5104, 1 mile from the city center.

REDLAND HOTEL
Owner: Teresa White
64 Hough Green
Chester CH4 8JY, England
Tel: (01244) 671024, Fax: (01244) 681309
Email: teresawhite@redlandhotel.fsnet.co.uk
12 rooms
£32.50–£42.50 per person
Open all year, Credit cards: none
Children welcome
www.karenbrown.com/england/redlandhotel.html

Chiddingfold, with its attractive homes set round the village green, is one of the most picturesque villages on the wooded Surrey Downs. A dovecote fronts the country lane just off the village green and a path leads beside it through a picture-book English cottage garden to Greenaway, the charming home of Sheila and John Marsh. The interior is just as delightful as the exterior, with low-ceilinged, beamed rooms, each decorated to perfection without making them stiffly formal or contrived. Guests enjoy the lovely living room with its views of the garden and part of Sheila and John's collection of colorful Staffordshire pottery displayed on the mantelshelf above the massive inglenook fireplace. Breakfast is served in the cozy, antique-filled dining room. Guests often walk down to one of the pubs on the village green for dinner. All bedrooms are in the original 17th-century, heavily beamed section of the house. The large front bedroom enjoys an old-fashioned bathroom with a claw-foot tub. The spacious French twin and a third small bedroom share a large, immaculate bathroom. Chiddingfold is conveniently located 40 miles from both Gatwick and Heathrow airports and London is less than an hour away by train. Guests often visit Petworth House, Bignor Roman villa, the Royal Horticultural Society gardens, Chichester, Portsmouth, and the south coast. *Directions:* From Guildford take the A3 and the A283 to Chiddingfold. Pickhurst Road is off the green and Greenaway is the third house on the left with the large dovecote in front.

GREENAWAY
Owners: Sheila & John Marsh
Pickhurst Road, Chiddingfold
Surrey GU8 4TS, England
Tel: (01428) 682920, Fax: (01428) 685078
Email: jfvmarsh@nildram.co.uk
3 rooms
£35–£40 per person
Open all year, Credit cards: MC, VS
Children welcome, No-smoking house
www.karenbrown.com/england/greenaway.html

Ashen Clough, Isobel and Norman Salisbury's home, began life in the 16th century as a prosperous yeoman's home set in a rural Derbyshire valley. Norman was for many years the local vet then retired to take on domestic duties, helping Isobel run their lovely home as the most welcoming of bed and breakfasts. Except on Sundays, guests dine with their hosts around the ancient refectory table in the low-beamed dining room. Drinks in the comfortable drawing room precede dinner and it is here that guests enjoy coffee and evening-long conversation before retiring to their delightful bedrooms. Country lanes lead to main roads that quickly transport you to Georgian Buxton with its restored opera house, Bakewell with its shops and Monday market, the Potteries where you can visit the Royal Crown Derby factories and factory shops, and the great houses of Chatsworth, Haddon, Keddleston, and Lyme Hall. *Directions:* From Buxton take the A6 (Manchester road) for 6 miles and at the roundabout turn left at the signpost for Chinley. Follow the B6062 into the village where you turn right and then right again into Maynestone Road. Ashen Clough is on your left after 1¼ miles.

ASHEN CLOUGH
Owners: Isobel & Norman Salisbury
Maynestone Road
Chinley, High Peak
Derbyshire SK23 6AH, England
Tel: (01663) 750311, Fax: none
Email: salisburys@talk21.com
3 rooms
£34–£37 per person, dinner £22 (not Sun)
Closed occasionally, Credit cards: none
Children over 12
www.karenbrown.com/england/chinley.html

A 16th-century Cotswold-stone house set in a picturesque village above Bourton-on-the-Water, Clapton Manor is surrounded by its carefully tended gardens in the shadow of St. James's church. Thick stone walls, exposed oak beams, mullioned windows, and inglenook fireplaces set the scene. William Fox, founder of the Sunday School Society, was lord of the manor and lived here in the 19th century. Two tastefully decorated double rooms have en-suite bathrooms, one of which is hidden behind a "secret" door. A cozy sitting room with comfy sofas, a wood fire, and books is available for less-than-perfect days. Breakfast is served either in the dining room, dominated by what is correctly described as a "depressed Tudor arch" fireplace or, weather permitting, outside on the terrace. Dinner is to be found at any of the many excellent pubs in the surrounding area. Karin and James, former Director of Design History at the Inchbald School of Garden Design, work together to plan, develop, and maintain the 1-acre garden, which they have lovingly replanted with old shrub roses, peonies, and autumn borders within a framework of hedges and dry-stone walls. Garden enthusiasts like to visit Kiftsgate and Hidcote. Shakespearean Stratford, the dreaming spires of Oxford, and Georgian Cheltenham are also popular destinations. *Directions:* Coming from Cirencester towards Stow on the A429, turn right at the Bourton Lodge hotel and follow signs for Clapton into the village. The manor is the three-story house on the left near the church.

CLAPTON MANOR   **New**
Owners: Karin & James Bolton
Clapton-on-the-Hill, Cheltenham
Gloucestershire GL54 2LG, England
Tel: (01451) 810202, Fax: (01451) 821804
2 rooms
£35–£45 per person
Closed Christmas & New Year, Credit cards: MC, VS
Children welcome, No-smoking house
www.karenbrown.com/england/clapton.html

This pretty village of flint-walled, tile-roofed cottages is no longer "next the sea," but separated from it by a vast saltwater marsh formed as the sea retreated. The massive structure of Cley Mill stands as a handsome monument to man's ability to harness the forces of nature. Guests enter the mill directly into the beamed dining room decorated with country-style pine furniture. The circular sitting room has large chintz chairs drawn round a stone fireplace whose mantel is a sturdy beam. Stacked above the sitting room are two large circular bedrooms with en-suite bathrooms: the Wheat Chamber is where the grain was stored and the Stone Room is where the massive grinding stones crushed the flour. I especially enjoyed my stay in the River Room with its private entrance but be aware that you can hear conversations in the kitchen. During the day the mill is open to the public to visit the observation room and the wooden cap of the mill with its massive gears and complex mechanisms that once turned the grinding stones. The old boathouse and stables in the yard have been converted into small, self-catering cottages. Birdwatching, sailing, cycling, and walking are popular pastimes in the area. The seaside towns of Sheringham, Cromer, and Wells are close at hand. There are a great many stately homes to explore such as Sandringham House, the Royal Family's country residence, Jacobean Fellbrigg Hall, Holkham, and Blickling Hall. *Directions:* From King's Lynn follow the A149 around the coast to Cley next the Sea, where the windmill is well signposted.

CLEY MILL GUEST HOUSE
Manager: Jeremy Bolan
Cley next the Sea, Holt
Norfolk NR25 7RP, England
Tel & fax: (01263) 740209
7 rooms
£36–£50 per person, dinner £17.50
Open all year, Credit cards: MC, VS
Children welcome
www.karenbrown.com/england/cleymillguesthouse.html

Manor Farm is a peaceful haven just inland from the sea, a glorious spot to enjoy once you have overcome the challenges of finding it. This part-whitewashed stone and slate manor is a splendid old building set in acres of glorious gardens. Muriel and Paul Knight operate on house party lines, with guests gathering for drinks and introductions before dinner at seven. The dinner party is an opportunity to meet people in a convivial manner and to enjoy a sociable evening in a very English setting. The antique furnishings, paintings, and decor reflect the age and ambiance of this Domesday-listed manor. Up one staircase are two lovely little cottagey rooms while up another are two equally delightful rooms. The scenery in this part of Cornwall is stunning and best enjoyed from the coastal path that meanders up and down the clifftops. Four miles away lies the strikingly picturesque harbor of Boscastle and just beyond it Tintagel with its legends of King Arthur. *Directions:* Ten miles south of Bude on the A39 turn right for Crackington Haven. At the sea front follow the same road up the other side of the valley and turn left into a narrow lane (Church Park Road) just before the red telephone box. Take the first right (Tinier Lane) and Manor Farm is in front of you after 300 yards.

MANOR FARM
Owners: Muriel & Paul Knight
Crackington Haven, near Bude
Cornwall EX23 0JW, England
Tel: (01840) 230304, Fax: none
4 rooms
£30–£35 per person, dinner £18*
*Not available in August
Open all year, Credit cards: none
No children, No-smoking house

Nancemellan is a beautiful Arts and Crafts home overlooking the rugged little bay of Crackington Haven, built in 1905 for a wealthy Londoner. Lorraine and Eddie have taken great pains to keep all the lovely old features of the house with its tiled entryway, beams, and ornate door and window moldings. Guests have a lovely drawing room where a log fire is lit on chilly evenings. Breakfast is the only meal served round the large pine table in the family kitchen. Lorraine chats to guests about where to go and what to see as she cooks on the Aga. For dinner, guests can go just down the road to the pub or Lorraine is happy to make dining arrangements at local farmhouses that specialize in offering dinner for visitors. A large double bedroom offers the most glorious of sea views and has its spacious bathroom, resplendent with claw-foot tub, just across the hall. The other double-bedded room has its bathroom (also with claw-foot tub) en suite while the twin-bedded room has an adjacent bathroom. Nine acres of gardens are yours to explore. The stunning views from the house tempt you out to the coastal path, which offers the most magnificent of vistas of this rocky part of Cornwall. To the north lies Clovelly while to the south you find Boscastle and Tintagel. *Directions:* Ten miles south of Bude on the A39 turn right for Crackington Haven. As the lane begins to drop steeply towards the sea, Nancemellan is on your right.

NANCEMELLAN
Owners: Lorraine & Eddie Ruff
Crackington Haven, near Bude
Cornwall EX23 0NN, England
Tel & fax: (01840) 230283
3 rooms
£22–£28 per person
Open Easter to Oct, Credit cards: none
Children over 12, No-smoking house

Just steps from the clifftops on a secluded stretch of Cornish coast, this 16th-century farmhouse snuggles in a hollow round a cobbled courtyard. The polished flagstone floors lead you into the comfortable sitting room with high-backed sofas grouped round the log-burning stove. Guests dine at separate tables and Gayle Crocker offers a hearty dinner with a choice of starter, main course, and dessert on Thursday, Friday, and Saturday nights. Farmhouse bedrooms range from snug to the spaciousness of room 2 with its carved oak bed. The farm is licensed for civil marriages—a romantic spot to "tie the knot." The adjacent barn houses an exhibition on the local flora and fauna. Gayle's brother Francis leads nature and badger walks. The clifftops provide magnificent views and a path leads to Strangles Beach where Thomas Hardy loved to walk with his first wife Emma. Walking the coastal path and the nearby villages of Boscastle and Tintagel are great attractions. *Directions:* From Bude, take the A39 towards Camelford and then turn right to Crackington Haven. At the beach, take the right-hand turn at the bottom of the hill for Trevigue and you find Trevigue Farm atop the cliffs after 2 miles.

TREVIGUE FARM
Owner: Gayle Crocker
Trevigue, near Crackington Haven
Bude
Cornwall EX23 0LQ, England
Tel & fax: (01840) 230418
3 rooms
£30–£36 per person, dinner £18*
*Thurs, Fri & Sat
Closed Christmas, Credit cards: none
Children over 12, No-smoking house

Folly Hill Cottage began life in the 1850s as a tiny farm cottage. Over the last 50 years every owner has added to the house and Sonia and John de Carle have done their bit with the addition of modern plumbing and more bathrooms. Guests enjoy breakfast in the snug breakfast room and, with advance notice, Sonia is happy to prepare a simple supper or more elaborate dinner on the night of your arrival (bring your own wine). Upstairs, a sitting nook provides a television, small refrigerator, books, and masses of information on the local area. A spacious twin-bedded room has a large bathroom and an alcove where you can prepare coffee and tea. The smaller bedroom has its private shower room across the hall. After a day of sightseeing enjoy a refreshing swim in the pool. The garden runs down to the river, which flows either side of the main lawn, formerly the tennis court for the "big house" up the road. Sissinghurst Castle with its lovely garden is nearby and guests often visit Canterbury and its famous cathedral, which is especially impressive during choral evensong. Leeds Castle, local vineyards, and the old railway at Tenterden are other popular attractions. *Directions:* Take the A21 south from Sevenoaks to the A262 signposted Goudhurst and Cranbrook. Pass the Kennel Holt Hotel on the right and a signpost for Colliers Green on the left. After 400 yards, turn left into Friezley Lane (between white posts). Go to the very end, up a small hill, and Folly Hill Cottage is the last house but one.

FOLLY HILL COTTAGE
Owners: Sonia & John de Carle
Friezley Lane, Hocker Edge
Cranbrook
Kent TN17 2LL, England
Tel & fax: (01580) 714299
2 rooms
£22–£24 per person, dinner £12.50–£17.50
Closed Christmas, Credit cards: none
Children over 10, No-smoking house

Everything about The Old Cloth Hall is exceptional, from the vast expanses of gardens with manicured lawns, roses, rhododendrons, and azaleas to the dignified old house, parts of which date back more than 500 years. Settle into the richly paneled drawing room with its commodious sofas and chairs drawn round the crackling log fire that blazes in the enormous inglenook. The Old Cloth Hall has been Katherine Morgan's home for many years and because it is a large house, she has an array of bedrooms that can be used for guest accommodation, which she prices by size and location. If you want to splurge, ask for The Four-Poster room and you will receive a king-size four-poster decked and draped in lemon-and-green-sprigged fabric with an enormous bathroom. The small downstairs twin is reserved for children. Elizabeth I came for lunch in 1573 but you can stay for dinner with your fellow guests. Guests are welcome to use the swimming pool and the tennis court. Sissinghurst Gardens are a mile away, while Sir Winston Churchill's home, Chartwell, Knole, Igtham Mote, Penshurt Place, and Batemans, Rudyard Kipling's home, are within easy reach. *Directions:* Take the A21 south from Sevenoaks, turn left at the A262 before Lamberhurst and right onto the A229. Go into Cranbrook and take a sharp left after the school. Follow this road for about a mile, bearing left when it forks, turn right just before the cemetery, and the entrance to The Old Cloth Hall is on your right.

THE OLD CLOTH HALL
Owner: Katherine Morgan
Cranbrook
Kent TN17 3NR, England
Tel & fax: (01580) 712220
3 rooms
£45–£55 per person, dinner £21
Closed Christmas, Credit cards: none
Children by arrangement
www.karenbrown.com/england/oldclothhall.html

This quiet, rural spot is just minutes from Scotch Corner on the A1, making it an ideal place to break your journey between the south of England and Scotland. David's family has always farmed in Yorkshire, and when he inherited this small farm, he moved here with Heather and built Clow Beck House. Heather and David are relaxed, welcoming people who truly enjoy sharing their home with visitors. Guests have a large formal drawing room but more often gravitate into the roomy country kitchen and the spacious beamed dining room with its cheery fire. After a day of sightseeing it's nice to stay home for dinner then stroll into the village for a drink. A couple of guestrooms are in the main house with the remainder occupying a stable, a granary, and cottage. (One room in the granary wing is equipped for the handicapped.) All the rooms are excellently fitted with TV, phone, bathrobes, and large umbrellas. Decor ranges from dramatic and colorful to simple and quiet. Where else can you enjoy a room swathed in orange, lime green, and buttercup yellow? Use this welcoming, off-the-beaten-tourist-path spot as a base for explorations to the Yorkshire Dales and Moors, and the heritage coast with Whitby, Robin Hood's Bay, and Runswick. Heather and David love planning routes for guests. *Directions:* From Scotch Corner go north on the A1 for a short distance to the Barton exit. Go through Barton and Newton Morell, turn right for Croft, and after 2½ miles turn left into the farm.

CLOW BECK HOUSE
Owners: Heather & David Armstrong
Monk End Farm
Croft on Tees, Darlington
North Yorkshire DL2 2SW, England
Tel: (01325) 721075, Fax: (01325) 720419
Email: heather@clowbeckhouse.co.uk
14 rooms
£40 per person, dinner £9–£20
Open all year, Credit cards: all major
Children welcome
www.karenbrown.com/england/clowbeckhouse.html

The Coach House is made up of a group of several old buildings, including a 1680s cottage and an old smithy, that form a square round a courtyard fronting directly on the A697 Coldstream to Morpeth road. The cottage serves as the dining room with two rooms either side of the entrance hall. Several of the nine bedrooms open directly onto the graveled courtyard—these are equipped for wheelchair access and each has a large open-plan bathroom. Most of the guestrooms have refrigerators and all have tea- and coffee-making facilities. A decadent afternoon tea of cakes and scones is laid in the high-beamed sitting room where French doors open onto the paved patio. Lynne offers an evening meal with a set main course and lots of choices of starters and dessert including several homemade ice creams. The decor is not perfect—a tad run-down in parts—but Lynn has made inroads into redecorating and there's a lot of warmth and atmosphere to the place. Crookham makes an ideal place to break the journey between Scotland and York, but several days spent here will allow you to explore the plethora of Northumbrian castles and battlefields (Flodden is just down the road) and the delightful Northumbrian coastline between Lindisfarne (Holy Island) and the ancient port of Seahouses. *Directions:* From the south take the A1 to Morpeth and the A697 (Coldstream road) for 35 miles to Crookham where you find The Coach House on the left about a mile after the right-hand turn for Ford and Etal.

THE COACH HOUSE
Owner: Lynne Anderson
Crookham, Cornhill on Tweed
Northumberland TD12 4TD, England
Tel: (01890) 820293, Fax: (01890) 820284
Email: stay@coachhousecrookham.com
9 rooms
£25–£39 per person, dinner £17.50
Open Easter to Oct, Credit cards: MC, VS (4% extra)
Children welcome
www.karenbrown.com/england/thecoachhouse.html

Crudwell is the most peaceful of rural villages just ten minutes north of the M4 between the historic towns of Cirencester and Malmesbury. Tucked behind the church and the ancient tithe barn where the granary for Malmesbury Abbey once stood you find Manor Farmhouse, a lovely honey-colored building set in a walled garden facing a paddock where cattle graze peacefully. Helen gives her guests a warm welcome, offering them tea or coffee on arrival and encouraging them to make themselves at home in the sitting room with its comfortable chairs and TV. The family bedroom with its prettily sprigged wallpaper has a double and single bed, idyllic views across the garden to the church, and an immaculate blue-and-white bathroom with both bath and shower across the hall. The spacious double bedroom at the front overlooks the paddock and tennis court (which guests are welcome to use) and has a spacious en-suite shower room. Helen is happy to provide dinner (with advanced notice), finding that guests often enjoy staying in and making themselves at home on the day of their arrival. There's a wealth of places and things to see—within an hour you can be in Oxford, Bristol, and Bath and there are enough gardens, historic homes, and quaint towns and villages in the area to keep you busy for a fortnight. *Directions:* Exit the M4 at junction 17 and take the A429 through Malmesbury towards Cirencester. In Crudwell turn right opposite The Plough, signposted Minety/Oaksey. Go straight then left between the church and the tithe barn.

MANOR FARMHOUSE
Owners: Helen & Philip Carter
Crudwell, Malmesbury
Wiltshire SN16 9ER, England
Tel: (01666) 577375, Fax: (01666) 823523
Email: user785566@aol.com
2 rooms
£27 per person, dinner £20
Closed Christmas & New Year, Credit cards: none
Children welcome, No-smoking house
www.karenbrown.com/england/manorfarmhouse.html

Delbury Hall, built in 1753, is one of the most beautiful Georgian houses in Shropshire, a grand red-brick edifice reflected in a lake with elegant swans. Despite its gracious architecture and lovely antiques, this is not an intimidating or overly grand house, but very much a home for Lucinda and Patrick Wrigley and their two young children. You enter directly into the imposing two-story entry hall with its staircase sweeping up to the gallery above. Here you find a four-poster room with a large en-suite bathroom and a suite of rooms with two bedrooms and a bathroom, which is often used for families. A spacious twin-bedded room has its private bathroom up a further flight of stairs. Guests help themselves to drinks at the honesty bar while Patrick prepares an elegant dinner with fruits and vegetables fresh from the garden. The lake includes a trout fishery where guests can try their hand at catching rainbow trout. Medieval Ludlow with its spectacular ruined castle and plethora of interesting antique shops is a ten-minute drive away. Other attractions include the Ironbridge Gorge museums and the Severn Valley Steam Railway. *Directions:* From Ludlow take the A49 north towards Shrewsbury and take the first right (B4365) signed Much Wenlock for 5 miles. Turn right on the B4368 to Diddlebury then right before the village at The Lodge for Delbury Hall. If you miss this turn, go into the village and follow signs for Delbury Trout Fishery.

DELBURY HALL
Owners: Patrick & Lucinda Wrigley
Diddlebury, near Craven Arms
Shropshire SY7 9DH, England
Tel: (01584) 841267, Fax: (01584) 841441
Email: wrigley@delbury.com
4 rooms
£55–£65 per person, dinner £35
Closed Christmas, Credit cards: MC, VS
Children welcome
www.karenbrown.com/england/delbury.html

Jackie's acres of garden have been voted among the top three in Somerset: plant-filled borders line the tumbling stream, the herbaceous border is ablaze with summer flowers, and the water meadow offers some unusual plant species. Jackie loves to share her beautiful home with guests who can choose from three very different bedrooms. The Cottage Suite offers a low-ceilinged bedroom, snug sitting room with television and sofas that can be made into extra beds, and a small bathroom. In contrast, the Master Suite offers a spacious high-ceilinged room with a queen-sized bed, television, and a large, luxurious Victorian-style bathroom. The Pine Bedroom takes its name from the enormous pine fitted cupboard that has been there since the house was built. For dinner try the Foresters Arms, just a two-minute walk away. There are ten classic gardens in South Somerset. Wells and Glastonbury are within easy touring distance, as is the Dorset Coast. *Directions:* From Yeovil, take the A30 (Crewkerne road) for 2 miles to the Yeovil Court Hotel. Turn immediately left at the signpost for North Coker, and Hardington. Pass the Foresters Arms, and Holywell House is the next driveway on the right. (Ignore all signposts for East Coker.)

HOLYWELL HOUSE
Owner: Jackie Somerville
Holywell
East Coker
Yeovil
Somerset BA22 9NQ, England
Tel: (01935) 862612, Fax: (01935) 863035
3 rooms
£32.50–£35 per person
Closed Christmas & New Year, Credit cards: none
Children welcome

Sitting in acres of glorious gardens, Old Whyly is the most gracious of 17th-century manor houses and home to Sarah Burgoyne and her sons, a home they love to share with their guests. Sarah has a gracious, easy way with her that soon has guests feeling at home. She encourages them to relax in the beautiful drawing room, sit in the garden, swim in the pool, or take a peaceful walk through adjacent farms. Guests gravitate to the long pine table in the huge farmhouse kitchen where Sarah loves to talk to them—except when she is involved in one of the more complicated dinner dishes. Cooking is a passion for Sarah and it would be a shame to stay here and not enjoy dinner with other guests at the large round dining table. Bedrooms are most attractive. Tulip offers the most spacious accommodation; French has blue toile wallpaper, drapes, and bedspread, and wisteria peeping in at the windows; Chinese has its large private bathroom across the hall. Old Whyly is perfect for opera fans as Glyndebourne is ten minutes away and hampers can be provided. Guests often visit Charleston Garden where the Bloomsbury set used to gather. Brighton is popular for its pavilion and interesting shops in the narrow lanes, while Nymans and Leonardslee are popular gardens. *Directions:* Take the A22 south from Uckfield past Halland for half a mile then take the first left off the large roundabout towards East Hoathly. After a quarter of a mile turn left into the drive by the post box. Where the drive divides into three, take the central gravel drive to Old Whyly.

OLD WHYLY
Owner: Sarah Burgoyne
East Hoathly
East Sussex BN8 6EL, England
Tel: (01825) 840216, Fax: (01825) 840738
3 rooms
£45 per person, dinner £22
Open all year, Credit cards: none
Children over 10
www.karenbrown.com/england/oldwhyly.html

Ely has a fascinating history. The town got its name when St. Dunstan found monks living with women—he didn't approve of that sort of behavior and turned them into eels. The cathedral with its huge tower held up by eight 64-ft oak trunks is visible from miles away. A short walk from this lovely building you find Cathedral House, home to Jenny and Robin Farndale. Built in the mid-1800s, the house's unusual design has the side facing directly onto the street while its front faces a spacious walled garden. I particularly enjoyed the Oriel Suite with its brass bed, claw-foot tub, and separate sitting room. If you are traveling with a child, opt for the family suite, which has both a single- and a double-bedded room and a bathroom. Breakfast is enjoyed round the pine farmhouse dining-room table where you can plan your day's excursions. For dinner there are several restaurants and pubs within walking distance, the most famous and popular being the adjacent Old Fire Engine House. If you are interested in self-catering accommodation, ask about the Coach House tucked away behind Cathedral House. It accommodates two to five persons and can be rented for partial or complete weeks. Ely is a perfect location for touring East Anglia—within an hour lie Cambridge, King's Lynn, Bury St. Edmunds, Wisbech, and Newmarket. *Directions:* Arriving in Ely, follow brown signs for the cathedral, pass the tourist office and The Old Engine House, on your right, and Cathedral House is the next house on your right. Park in front on the gravel.

CATHEDRAL HOUSE
Owners: Jenny & Robin Farndale
17 St. Mary's Street, Ely
Cambridgeshire CB7 4ER, England
Tel & fax: (01353) 662124
Email: farndale@cathedralhouse.co.uk
3 rooms, 1 cottage
£30–£35 per person (2-night minimum on weekends)
Cottage: £700 weekly
Closed Christmas & New Year, Credit cards: none
Children over 12, No-smoking house
www.karenbrown.com/england/cathedral.html

Legend has it that the French King John II was taken prisoner by the Black Prince and held captive here in 1356. Dating back to Jacobean times and substantially expanded thereafter, the house has been carefully restored by the Cunninghams, who have retained many of the original architectural features such as stone and inglenook fireplaces, stone mullioned windows with leaded lights, and heavy beams. Four bedrooms—Jacobean, Tudor, or Victorian—are available, all with either en-suite or private bathrooms and all comfortably furnished with a liberal mix of brass beds and antiques. A small family annex in the roof is linked to the Tudor room—very handy for those traveling with children. Breakfast is served in the Elizabethan dining room or on the terrace with Percy the peacock and views of the manicured lawn, lily pond, and the wild garden beyond with its rose walk. Guests are welcome to use the all-weather tennis court or swim in the pool. On days less conducive to outdoor activities retire to the Edwardian sitting room complete with pool table or the quieter sitting room with its log fire. There are famous gardens galore nearby: just up the road is Scotney Castle, and Batemans, Great Dixter, Sissinghurst, Pashley Manor, and Merriments are all within an hour's drive. Of course, you must visit Churchill's home, Chartwell. *Directions:* Go west off the A21 onto the A265 at Hurst Green. At the end of the village fork right (Burgh Hill) then turn right again into Sheep Street Lane. The house is 1 mile farther on the left

KING JOHN'S LODGE   **New**
Owners: Jill & Richard Cunningham
Sheep Street Lane
Etchingham, Sussex TN19 7AZ, England
Tel: (01580) 819232, Fax: (01580) 819562
4 rooms
£35–£40 per person, dinner £25
Closed Christmas & New Year, Credit cards: none
Children welcome

The tiny village of Fordham is just outside Newmarket, the horseracing capital of England. Naturally, a lot of racing types live hereabouts and no one is more passionate about all things equine than Malcolm Roper. He arranges and conducts day-long tours that take guests to early-morning gallop watching, round the trainers' yards, and visiting the studs. Another of his tours is designed specifically for Dick Francis fans, visiting the places he mentions in his books. Back at home, wife Jan takes care of guests, always ready with a smile, a pot of tea, and a chat. She prides herself on having the two bedrooms in the house equipped with everything from a hairdryer and trouser press to a television. I especially liked the spacious twin-bedded room (beds can be zipped together) with its stripped-pine woodwork and furniture—its private bathroom is across the hall. Jan often rents this room to families in conjunction with an additional small double-bedded room. A delightful queen-bedded room has a tiny en-suite shower room. For complete privacy (at less expensive rates) Jan has three simply furnished rooms (one en suite, two sharing a shower room) in an adjacent converted barn. Breakfast, the only meal served, is enjoyed in summer in the Victorian conservatory overlooking the garden. Cambridge and Ely are within easy reach. *Directions:* From Newmarket take the A142 towards Ely through Fordham. Turn right on Murfitts Lane, at the end turn right into Carter Street, and Queensberry is on the left, after half a mile, next to Fordham Moor Road.

QUEENSBERRY
Owners: Jan & Malcolm Roper
196 Carter Street
Fordham
Cambridgeshire CB7 5JU, England
Tel: (01638) 720916, Fax: (01638) 720233
5 rooms
£25–£30 per person
Closed Christmas, Credit cards: none
Children welcome, No-smoking house

When Mary and Tony Dakin bought The Old Parsonage at an auction, it was in a sad state of disrepair and they have put a great deal of work into making it the lovely home you see today. In the days when clerics were men of substance, there were six servants for the house and garden, but now it's just Mary, Tony, their two sons, and the tractor-mower. In the morning, Tony cooks breakfast while Mary assists guests. Typical of grand Georgian houses, the rooms are tall and spacious and the Dakins have furnished them in a most delightful manner. Two of the bedrooms have double-bedded four-posters while the other two rooms are twin-bedded. One of the twin-bedded rooms is in a much older section of the house and is more cottagey in size. Two bedrooms have spacious bathrooms with large tubs and separate showers. Tony is a keen gardener—the sunny conservatory is always full of plants—and photographer—photos of longtime village residents line the hallway and historic Frant pictures, together with Mary's tapestries of village scenes, adorn the dining room. Frant is a most attractive village set round a green, with two pubs where guests usually go for dinner. Information folders in the bedrooms give details on the 15 houses, castles, and gardens to visit in the area. London is a 50-minute train ride from Frant station. *Directions:* From Tunbridge Wells, take the A267 south for 2½ miles to Frant. Turn left at the 30 mph Frant sign, and The Old Parsonage is on your left, just before the church.

THE OLD PARSONAGE
Owners: Mary & Tony Dakin
Church Lane, Frant, Tunbridge Wells
Kent TN3 9DX, England
Tel & fax: (01892) 750773
Email: oldparson@aol.com
4 rooms
£36–£44 per person
Open all year, Credit cards: MC, VS
Children over 7, No smoking house
www.karenbrown.com/england/theoldparsonage.html

The soothing sound of water splashing down the mill race is the only sound that breaks the countryside peace and quiet when you stay at Maplehurst Mill, the site of a mill since 1309. Heather feels that eating here is an integral part of the stay and guests dine by candlelight in the ancient miller's house with its beams and inglenook fireplace. Bottomend, a ground-floor bedroom, sits directly above the mill race and its windows open onto the moss-covered millwheel. Topend, at the top of the mill, has a beamed bathroom and the four-poster room, which overlooks the meadows, has its beds legs different heights to allow for the sloping floor. The room across the garden in the stables lacks the warm country character of those in the mill. A heated swimming pool overlooks the fields. Idencroft Herb Gardens are just round the corner and Brattle Farm, an old-fashioned working farm, is an excellent choice for those who have visited all Kent's castles, gardens, and stately homes. *Directions:* From the M20 take the A229 Hastings exit and follow Hastings signs through Maidstone for 12 miles to Staplehurst. At the end of the village turn left into the Frittenden road. After 1¼ miles, opposite a white house, turn right into a narrow lane. At the end turn right and you'll find the mill at the foot of the incline.

MAPLEHURST MILL
Owners: Heather & Kenneth Parker
Mill Lane
Frittenden
Kent TN17 2DT, England
Tel: (01580) 852203, Fax: (01580) 852117
Email: maplehurst@clara.net
5 rooms
£32–£38 per person, dinner £24
Open all year, Credit cards: MC, VS
Children over 12, No-smoking house
www.karenbrown.com/england/maplehurstmill.html

With its acres of lovely gardens, grass tennis court, and heated swimming pool, Ennys is an idyllic, 17th-century manor house set deep in the Cornish countryside, 3 miles from St. Michael's Mount. You reach it along a private lane, and I timed my arrival perfectly—the kettle had just boiled, and I settled down for afternoon tea in the spacious country-pine kitchen. Polished flagstones line the hallway leading to the comfortable sitting room with its sofas drawn round the fire and mementos of Gill's extensive travels. Breakfast is the only meal served but Gill is happy to make reservations at local inns and restaurants for dinner. Upstairs are three lovely bedrooms, two of them delectable four-posters. Families are welcome in the suites, which occupy an adjacent barn—bedrooms here are also delightfully appointed, though without the bric-a-brac that can be so hazardous to children. Gill has three architect-designed self-catering cottages for longer stays. St. Michael's Mount is a "must visit." A delightful day trip involves an hour's walk (or a short drive) to the station to take a train to St. Ives to visit the Tate Gallery, which displays the work of 20th-century St. Ives artists. *Directions:* From Exeter, take the A30 to Crowlas village (4 miles before Penzance). Turn towards Helston on the A394 and at the next roundabout turn left for Relubbus. Go through Goldsithney and St. Hilary, and when the Ennys's signpost is on the right, turn left and follow Trewhella lane to the house.

ENNYS
Owner: Gill Charlton
St. Hilary, Goldsithney, Penzance
Cornwall TR20 9BZ, England
Tel: (01736) 740262, Fax: (01736) 740055
Email: ennys@ennys.co.uk
5 rooms, 3 cottages
£30–£37.50 per person
Open mid-Feb to mid-Nov, Credit cards: MC, VS
Children over 3 welcome in family suites
www.karenbrown.com/england/ennysfarm.html

Ashfield House sits on a quiet little courtyard just off Grassington's main street. I loved this 17th-century house from the moment I stepped through the low doorway into the quaint little parlor where an old polished settle sits beside a massive log-burning fireplace. Another small sitting room has groupings of chairs and an honesty bar where guests enjoy a drink before going into the little cottagey dining room for one of Keith's set three-course dinners with choices of starters and dessert. (In the spring dinner is not served on Saturdays, for the rest of the year it is not served on Wednesdays and Saturdays.) In winter and spring when guests return earlier from sightseeing and walking, Linda and Keith also offer scones and tea at 4:30 pm. The bedrooms open up beyond their low doors and some are quite spacious. Two have lovely views of the garden while one has a close-up view of the adjacent cottage but the advantage of a larger bathroom. All bedrooms have compact shower rooms, TVs, and tea-making facilities. To experience some magnificent scenery, take a breathtaking circular drive from Grassington and back again through Littondale, over the fells to Malham Cove, and back to the village. *Directions:* From Skipton take the B6265 to Grassington. Turn into the main street, pass the cobbled square, and turn sharp left after the Devonshire Hotel onto a cobbled access road that leads to Ashfield House.

ASHFIELD HOUSE
Owners: Linda & Keith Harrison
Grassington, Skipton
North Yorkshire BD23 5AE, England
Tel & fax: (01756) 752584
Email: info@ashfieldhouse.co.uk
7 rooms
£30–£34 per person, dinner £17*
*Not Sat, also not Wed most of year (see above)
Open Feb to Christmas, Credit cards: MC, VS
Children over 5, No-smoking house
www.karenbrown.com/england/ashfield.html

Church House, a spacious Georgian home, has a sweep of driveway circling to the front door beneath massive copper beeches. To the rear are lawns, sheep pasture, and a helicopter landing pad for those who care to arrive by air. Guests have a high-ceilinged, comfortable yellow drawing room where Anna displays her collection of paintings by West-Country artist Reg Gammon. Anna is happy, with advance notice, to prepare dinner. Guests eat together round the long polished table and you are welcome to bring your own wines. A graceful wooden staircase spirals its way up to the top floor and the homey guestrooms. The largest bedroom has its private bathroom across the hall while the other three rooms have their facilities in the room, artfully concealed behind tall wooden screens. Ask for the one with the view from the loo of Grittleton rooftops. On the landing is an information table showing all the things to do and see in the area, though guests are welcome to spend their days relaxing around the heated swimming pool. Grittleton is well placed to visit Bath, Bristol, Malmesbury, Tetbury, and the picture-perfect village of Castle Combe. Every May the Badminton horse trials are held nearby. *Directions:* Exit the M4 at junction 17, taking the A429 towards Cirencester, and almost immediately (at the crossroads) turn left for the 3½-mile drive to Grittleton. Church House is beside the church.

CHURCH HOUSE
Owners: Anna & Michael Moore
Grittleton, Chippenham
Wiltshire SN14 6AP, England
Tel: (01249) 782562, Fax: (01249) 782546
Email: moore@flydoc.fsbusiness.co.uk
4 rooms
£31 per person, dinner £21
Open all year, Credit cards: none
Children under 2 & over 12
www.karenbrown.com/england/churchhouse.html

Surrounded by a sky-wide landscape of fields, this converted 19th-century oast offers spacious accommodation within a half hour's drive of Kent's most celebrated tourist attractions. The lower half of the roundels, where the hops were roasted, has been converted into a spacious sitting room, but, more often than not, guests gather in the open-plan kitchen, which was formerly a barn. Anne is happy to provide dinner with advance notice. Two bedrooms (a twin and a double) occupy the upper reaches of the roundels and share a well-equipped bathroom. The third bedroom is very large and has its bathroom en suite. Alexei, the friendly golden retriever, is a great favorite with guests. Anne gives her guests lists of places to visit and a map of pubs and restaurants in the area to assist them in making sightseeing and dining decisions. Nearby places of interest include Chartwell (Churchill's home), 13th-century Hever Castle, the onetime home of the Boleyn family, and Penshurst Place, a 14th-century manor house. *Directions:* From Tonbridge, take the A26 towards Maidstone. After the village of Hadlow, pass Leavers Manor Hotel on the right and turn right into Stanford Lane. Leavers Oast is the third driveway on your right.

LEAVERS OAST
Owners: Anne & Denis Turner
Stanford Lane
Hadlow
Tonbridge
Kent TN11 0JN, England
Tel & fax: (01732) 850924
Email: denis@leavers-oast.freeserve.co.uk
3 rooms
£27.50–£31 per person, dinner £22
Open all year, Credit cards: none
Children over 12, No-smoking house
www.karenbrown.com/england/leaversoast.html

There are many good reasons to visit Leicestershire and this exceptional home at the edge of a peaceful village with many picturesque thatched cottages is one of them. Here old furniture is polished till it gleams, the windows sparkle, and everything is in apple-pie order. The evening sun streams into the drawing room where books on stately homes and castles invite browsing. Breakfast is served in a small dining room with a long trestle table. If there are several people for dinner, Raili (who grew up in Finland) sets the elegant table in the large dining room and serves a variety of meals using organic vegetables from her garden. The principal bedroom has en-suite facilities, while the other guestrooms have either private bathrooms or shower rooms. Bedrooms have televisions and someone is always on hand to make a pot of tea. A three-day Christmas program gives guests the opportunity to experience a quiet, traditional English country Christmas—visits to the hunt and the midnight carol service are highlights. Nearby are a great many stately homes (Burghley House and Rockingham Castle, for instance), lots of antique shops, cathedrals at Ely and Peterborough, historic towns (Stamford and Uppingham), and ancient villages. *Directions:* From Uppingham take the A47 and turn left at East Norton for Hallaton. Drive through the village and The Old Rectory is next to the church.

THE OLD RECTORY
Owners: Raili & Tom Fraser
Hallaton, Market Harborough
Leicestershire LE16 8TY, England
Tel & fax: (01858) 555350
3 rooms
£35 per person, dinner £15
Open all year, Credit cards: none
Children over 7, No-smoking house
www.karenbrown.com/england/hallaton.html

Hamsterley Forest, a vast woodland with clearings and streams nestling beneath wide expanses of moorland 40 miles south of Hadrian's Wall, is a noted beauty spot. Helene's grandparents used to love walking here and were so captivated by the tranquil setting of the grand crumbling hunting lodge they found that they moved in and set about its complete restoration. Now the house is divided into three and Helene is fortunate enough to occupy the largest section with its high-ceilinged baronial dining room. Guests gather here for a delicious five-course dinner (bring your own wine). Upstairs, the large front bedroom has a huge bathroom with sunken tub, while the pink and blue rooms are small only by comparison. Should you tire of walking, Raby Castle, Bowes Museum, and Killhope Wheel (a mining museum) are all nearby. Beamish Open Air Museum, Hadrian's Wall, and Durham Cathedral make popular day trips. It's a perfect place to take a few days' break on the way to or from Scotland. *Directions:* Leave the A1 at Darlington and take the A68 towards Consett for 15 miles where you turn left at the brown signs for Hamsterley Forest (2 miles after Toft Hill). Go through Hamsterley village (ignore forest signs) and continue for 2 miles, turning right at the sign "The Grove." Follow the road left then take the next right into the forest at the Grove House signpost. After 3 miles go over a stone bridge—the house faces you.

GROVE HOUSE
Owners: Helene & Russell Close
Hamsterley Forest, Bishop Auckland
Co Durham DL13 3NL, England
Tel: (01388) 488203, Fax: (01388) 488174
Email: xov47@dial.pipex.com
3 rooms
£26.50–£32.50 per person, dinner £20.50
Closed mid-Dec to mid-Jan, Credit cards: none
Children over 8, No-smoking house
www.karenbrown.com/england/grovehouse.html

Surrounded by lush green fields, Greenlooms Cottage offers a quiet countryside location just 5 miles from the heart of medieval Chester. The cottage was the hedger-and-ditcher's cottage on the Duke of Westminster's Eaton estate. Hezekiah, the last incumbent, lived here for many years with his sister Miriam who raised pigs and geese. Now Greenlooms is home to Deborah and Peter Newman who have sympathetically extended and modernized the cottage, while keeping all its lovely old features such as the low, beamed ceilings and the pump in the garden. Step through the front door into the old-fashioned pine country kitchen where Deborah serves breakfast. Through the snug television room you come to the cottagey little bedrooms. For dinner, Deborah usually suggests the Grosvenor Arms in Aldford or dining in the atmospheric bar at nearby Willington Hall. Rather than looking for parking in the center of Chester, drive to the Park and Ride from where a shuttle bus transports you into town (runs every ten minutes till 6 pm). Conwy Castle and Bodnant Gardens in Wales are a very popular day trip. *Directions:* From Chester take the A41 (Whitchurch road) south for 2 miles, and turn left at Whitehouse Antiques (before the Black Dog pub). Follow the road through the village for 1½ miles, turn right into Martins Lane, and Greenlooms Cottage is on your right, after less than a mile.

GREENLOOMS COTTAGE
Owners: Deborah & Peter Newman
Hargrave
Chester
Cheshire CH3 7RY, England
Tel: (01829) 781475, Fax: none
Email: greenloom@talk21.com
2 rooms
£25–£30 per person, dinner £15
Open all year, Credit cards: none
Children welcome, No-smoking house
www.karenbrown.com/england/greenlooms.html

Built in the 14th and 15th centuries with 20th-century additions, The Hatch, painted a delectable shade of ice-cream orange, has upper-story bedroom windows peeping out from beneath a steep thatched roof. This idyllic exterior is complemented by its welcoming owners, Bridget and Robin Oaten, and the most attractive of interiors furnished with lovely antiques. Guests have a cozy, beamed sitting room with a sofa and chairs grouped round a huge fireplace. Breakfast is the only meal served in the adjacent dining room with its ancient steep staircase leading upstairs to a cottage-cozy queen bedroom and its darling en-suite bathroom. The adjacent sweet little single room is available for a child or can be used to form a suite of rooms for friends traveling together. Beyond the kitchen lies a very spacious twin-bedded room with French windows opening to a private patio overlooking the apple orchard and fields. This bedroom has the added bonus of a small kitchen, spacious, immaculate bathroom, and a private entry. Long Melford with its two stately homes and plethora of antique shops is a popular nearby town to visit, as is Lavenham with its ancient Guildhall. Bury St. Edmunds, Ely, and Cambridge are also popular destinations. *Directions:* From Bury St. Edmunds take the A143 south towards Haverhill and turn left on the B1066 signposted Glemsford. After 6 miles turn left at the cluster of cottages—The Hatch is the first house down the lane on the right. If you find yourself at the village green, you have gone too far.

THE HATCH
Owners: Bridget & Robin Oaten
Pilgrims Lane
Cross Green, Hartest
Suffolk IP29 4ED, England
Tel & fax: (01284) 830226
3 rooms
£30–£35 per person
Closed Christmas, Credit cards: none
Children over 9, No-smoking house

It was love at first sight when I came upon Carr Head Farm sitting high above Hathersage village with steep crags and windswept heather moors as a backdrop. The garden presents a large flagstone patio, a profusion of flowers nestled in little niches in the terraces leading down to a sweeping lawn, and the most spectacular view across this beautiful Derbyshire valley. The beauty of Mary Bailey's gardens is matched by the loveliness of her home where everything has been done with caring and impeccable taste. The beamed dining room is furnished in period style with groupings of tables and chairs where guests gather for breakfast, the only meal served. The adjacent drawing room is very elegant in blues and creams, a bowl of sweets sitting on the coffee table next to a stack of interesting books. The two lovely bedrooms have en-suite bathrooms. The larger bedroom offers beautiful views of the valley. The Peak District with its picturesque villages, stone-walled fields, and dramatic dales is on your doorstep, as are Haddon Hall and Chatsworth House. *Directions:* Exit the M1 at junction 29 towards Baslow where you take the A623 to the B6001, through Grindleford to Hathersage. At the junction with the main road, turn right up the village, left into School Lane, and first left. Just before the church (Little John of Robin Hood fame has his grave in the churchyard) turn right up Church Bank to the farm.

CARR HEAD FARM
Owners: Mary & Michael Bailey
Church Bank
Hathersage
Hope Valley S32 1BR, England
Tel: (01433) 650383, Fax: (01433) 651441
2 rooms
£30 per person
Closed Christmas, Credit cards: none
Children over 12, No-smoking house

Sheltered in a gentle fold of the hills beneath the spectacular crags of Haytor Rocks, Haytor Vale is a quiet village made up of little cottages and The Rock Inn. With its wooden beams and huge open fireplace, the inn has a cozy, traditional ambiance. The food here is delightful: fish specials are posted on the board and lots of choices are offered on the menu. You can eat in the bar or choose from several snug little rooms (all but the bar are no-smoking). All the bedrooms, which are named after horses that have won the Grand National, have televisions (including a movie channel), tea and coffee, telephones, and mini bars. Highland Wedding, Sheila's Cottage, and Lovely Cottage are all larger rooms with both bath and shower. A relatively small supplement is charged for these deluxe rooms, and it is well worth paying. Lovely Cottage has an old oak four-poster bed and a dark-beamed ceiling. From the giant rocky outcrop of neighboring Haytor Rocks you can see the vast extent of Dartmoor National Park, the Teign estuary, and the rolling hills of southern Devon. The nearby quarry supplied the stone used for building London Bridge, which now resides in America. *Directions:* Take the M5 from Exeter, which joins the A38, Plymouth road, then the A382 to Bovey Tracey. At the first roundabout turn left and follow the road up to Haytor and cross a cattle grid onto the moor. At the red telephone box, turn left into Haytor Vale.

THE ROCK INN
Owner: Christopher Graves
Haytor Vale,
Newton Abbot, Devon TQ13 9XP, England
Tel: (01364) 661305, Fax: (01364) 661242
Email: rockinn@eclipse.co.uk
9 rooms
£36–£48 per person, dinner from £15
Open all year, Credit cards: AX, VS
Children welcome
www.karenbrown.com/england/rockinn.html

Helm is a scattering of farmhouses sitting high on the open hillside offering magnificent views of Wensleydale. On the far right of this group of houses you find the 17th-century farmhouse also called Helm—John and Barbara's home. A colony of doves in the ornamental dovecote adds to the charm of the place. A tiny entrance hall brings you into the stone-flagged dining room with its beamed ceiling (there are over 40 choices of wine with dinner). At the bottom of the little staircase you find a massive stone cheese press, which was formerly used in the farmhouse for the production of Wensleydale cheese. Two delightful bedrooms, a twin and a double, facing the front of the house have panoramic dales views and compact shower rooms. A third bedroom, a very snug and cozy double room, faces the rear of the house and has a larger bathroom with a Victorian tub. The nearby Kings Arms pub has an old-fashioned bar that appeared as the Drovers Arms in the James Herriot television series. A short walk over the fields brings you to the dramatic waterfalls of Whitfield Gill and Mill Gill. Farther afield lies the village of Hawes where you can visit the Wensleydale Creamery to watch cheese being produced. *Directions:* Take the A684 through Wensleydale to Bainbridge. Cross the river (signposted for Askrigg) and immediately after going round a sharp right-hand bend turn left (small signpost for Helm) up a narrow lane that goes up steeply into open countryside to the hamlet of Helm.

HELM
Owners: Barbara & John Drew
Helm, Askrigg, near Leyburn
North Yorkshire DL8 3JF, England
Tel & fax: (01969) 650443
Email: holiday@helmyorkshire.com
3 rooms
£32–£39 per person, dinner £19.50–£22.50
Closed Nov to Jan 2, Credit cards: MC, VS
Children over 10, No-smoking house
www.karenbrown.com/england/helmcountryhouse.html

This timbered pink house and its black-painted wooden barn hug a quiet country road on the edge of the peaceful Suffolk village of Higham. Meg Parker, with her gentle Dalmatian, Crumpet, at her heels, offers a warm smile and a sincere welcome to her home, quickly putting visitors at ease. Meg leads her guests to the lovely drawing room and then escorts them up the broad staircase to their rooms. Breakfast is enjoyed around the large dining-room table and, since it is the only meal served, she is happy to offer advice on where to dine, often suggesting The Angel at Stoke by Nayland. Bedrooms vary in size from large twin-bedded rooms to a cozy double room, in the oldest part of the house, with an en-suite bathroom. Outside, Meg's large garden is carefully tended and stretches towards the River Brett where a punt and a canoe are available for guests' use. The narrow Brett soon becomes the broader Stour and you can punt/paddle upstream for a picnic and idly drift home or go downstream to Stratford St. Mary and work off a lunch at The Swan by making your way back upstream. A swimming pool is tucked into one sheltered corner of the garden and a well-kept tennis court occupies another. A highlight of a stay here is to visit Flatford, immortalized in the paintings of John Constable. *Directions:* Leave the A12 between Colchester and Ipswich at Stratford St. Mary. The Old Vicarage is 1 mile to the west next to the church.

THE OLD VICARAGE
Owner: Meg Parker
Higham, Colchester
Suffolk CO7 6JY, England
Tel: (0120) 6337248, Fax: none
Email: oldvic.higham@bushinternet.com
3 rooms
£26–£30 per person
Open all year, Credit cards: none
Children welcome
www.karenbrown.com/england/oldvichigham.html

Horsleygate Hall nestles in the sheltered Cordwell Valley at the edge of the Peak District National Park. The hall was built in 1783 as a farmhouse and later extended in 1836. Margaret and Robert have been careful to preserve all its old features such as the old farmhouse kitchen with its blackened Yorkshire range, flagstone floors, and the old pine woodwork and doors. Guests have a comfortable, homey sitting room and enjoy breakfast in the old schoolroom next door. Visitors often go to the Trout Inn in Barlow or the Robin Hood in Holmesfield for dinner. The attractive, spacious bedrooms enjoy views of the magnificent garden and superb Peak District scenery. The lovely garden contains many enchanting treasures: terraces, flower-filled borders, rock gardens, pools, and woodland paths. A grand garden on an infinitely larger scale surrounds Chatsworth House, the enormous home of the Duke and Duchess of Devonshire, which is full of opulent rooms and priceless paintings and furniture. Haddon Hall, a romantic, 14th-century manor house, has a fragrant rose garden. Bakewell, Ilam, Edensor, Hartington, Ashford-in-the-Water, and Eyam are particularly attractive villages in this area. *Directions:* Leave the M1 motorway at junction 29 into Chesterfield where you take the B6051 (Hathersage) through Barlow and Millthorpe, then take the first turn right (Horsleygate Lane) and immediately left into Horsleygate Hall's driveway.

HORSLEYGATE HALL
Owners: Margaret & Robert Ford
Horsleygate Lane
Holmesfield, near Chesterfield
Derbyshire S18 7WD, England
Tel: (0114) 2890333, Fax: none
3 rooms
£23–£25 per person
Closed Christmas, Credit cards: none
Children over 5, No-smoking house

The first thing you notice when you come through Woodhayes's front door is the portraits, huge paintings that sometimes stretch from floor to ceiling. Once you have made yourself at home in this friendly house, you may be inclined, as I was, to do a "who's who" of Noel's forbears, ascertaining how the congenial pictures in your room are related to all the others. Guests dine by candlelight round the polished dining-room table in what was at one time the home's kitchen—hence the flagstone floors and huge inglenook fireplace, which now contains a wood-burning stove. The twin-bedded room at the front of the house has commanding views across the valley while the four-poster room overlooks the rose garden at the side of the house. Both have en-suite bathrooms. A single bedroom has its private bathroom down the hall. Dumpdon Celtic hill fort rises behind the house and beyond lies the rolling green of the Blackdown Hills, a wonderful place for walking. Nearby Honiton is the historic center for lace making and a small museum chronicles the industry's history and development. A 20-minute drive brings you to the Victorian resort of Sidmouth and Beer, a fishing village in a little bay. *Directions:* Woodhayes is prominently visible on high ground 1½ miles northeast of Honiton. Take the Dunkeswell road, cross the River Otter, and take the first turn right. Woodhayes's drive is the first on the left.

WOODHAYES
Owners: Christy & Noel Page-Turner
Honiton
Devon EX14 0TP, England
Tel & fax: (01404) 42011
Email: cmpt@inweb.co.uk
3 rooms
£37 per person, dinner £24
Closed Feb, Credit cards: MC, VS
Children over 12
www.karenbrown.com/england/woodhayes.html

The rector of Hopesay was quite the lord of the manor, with most of the buildings in this tiny hamlet falling under his domain: the 12th-century church of St. Mary, the grand, 17th-century rectory, servants' cottages, stables, barns, and a school. Parishioners came from outlying farms and villages. However grand the former rector's lifestyle may have been, the house can never have looked lovelier than it does today. Relax by the log fire in the beautiful drawing room and admire the garden vista of mature copper beeches, Norway maples, azaleas, and rhododendrons. Enjoy a lovely dinner and breakfast round the long refectory table overlooking Hopesay Hill. Equally delightful views are offered from the three very attractively decorated bedrooms. There are excellent country walks from the house and locally to Offa's dyke and the Long Mynd. Historical remains, hill forts, and castles abound (nearby Stokesay and Ludlow are a must). Guests often spend a day visiting the Ironbridge Gorge museums, while antiquers head to Ludlow and Shrewsbury. *Directions:* Leave the A49 at Craven Arms and take the B4368 to Clun. At Aston-on-Clun turn right over a small humpback bridge by the Flag Tree (literally a tree festooned with flags). The Old Rectory is on your left, next to the church, after 1 mile.

THE OLD RECTORY
Owners: Roma & Michael Villar
Hopesay
Craven Arms
Shropshire SY7 8HD, England
Tel: (01588) 660245, Fax: (01588) 660502
3 rooms
£37.50 per person, dinner £22.50
Closed Christmas & New Year, Credit cards: none
Children over 12, No-smoking house

Behind the tile-hung façade of Rixons lies a home that dates back to Tudor times, full of beams and low ceilings, with an inglenook fireplace and a snug, paneled study. Enjoy breakfast round the long refectory table and chat with Geoffrey and Jean about the local pubs that they recommend for dinner. The galleried guestroom is open to the rafters with its bedroom downstairs and a sitting room and the bathroom on the balcony above. Honey-colored beams, country-pine furniture, and sprigged bedcovers make the twin-bedded room, tucked under the eaves, a delight. Horsted Keynes has a lovely old church built as a replica of one in Cahagnes, France by a Norman nobleman after the Battle of Hastings. There are two village pubs serving food a few minutes' walk away. On weekends and in the summer, vintage steam trains run between Horsted Keynes and Sheffield Park, which is especially beautiful in spring. Other lovely gardens include Nymans, Leonardslee, and Wakehurst Place. *Directions:* From the M25 take the M23 south, exiting at junction 10 on the A264 towards East Grinstead. At the second roundabout turn right on the B2028 and go about 6 miles through Ardingly. Take the left turning signposted Horsted Keynes and Danehill. In Horsted Keynes turn right into the Lewes Road—Rixons is the second house on the right.

RIXONS
Owners: Jean & Geoffrey Pink
Lewes Road
Horsted Keynes
West Sussex RH17 7DP, England
Tel: (01825) 790453, Fax: none
2 rooms
£35 per person
Closed Christmas & New Year, Credit cards: none
Children over 12, No-smoking house

Set in a valley carved by a stream rushing down from high, bleak moorlands, Hutton le Hole is a cluster of pale stone houses, a picturesque village in the heart of the spectacular North Yorkshire Moors National Park. The lintel above the Hammer and Hand's doorway declares the date of the house, built as a beer house for the ironworkers, as 1784. Now it is home to Ann, a journalist, and John, once a London policeman, and their family, who happily welcome visitors to their guesthouse. Dinner is available Friday to Monday, served in a small paneled dining room. The gentle tick of a huge grandfather clock and the crackle of a blazing log fire welcome you to the sitting room, where a television is available for guests' use. A steep, narrow staircase leads to three snug bedrooms, each prettily decorated. Additional bedrooms are found in the adjacent cottage. Hutton le Hole is home to the Ryedale Folk Museum, which is well worth a visit. York is less than an hour's drive away. *Directions:* Take the A170 from Thirsk towards Pickering. The left-hand turn to Hutton le Hole is signposted just after Kirbymoorside. The Hammer and Hand is at the heart of the village.

HAMMER AND HAND GUEST HOUSE
Owners: Ann & John Wilkins
Hutton le Hole
York
North Yorkshire YO62 6UA, England
Tel: (01751) 417300, Fax: (01751) 417711
Email: info@hammerandhandhouse.com
7 rooms
£25–£30 per person, dinner £15 (Fri to Mon)
Open all year, Credit cards: MC, VS
Children welcome, No-smoking house
www.karenbrown.com/england/hammer.html

The highlight of a stay at the Old Windmill is to experience the welcome and gracious hospitality of its resident owners, Sheila and Mike Dale. Set on a tranquil 2-acre parcel, this interesting old building's structure and character have evolved with its various uses. It originated as a mill during the 1840s and the turret-like tower still dominates the structure. In 1906 it was converted to a residence with the dramatic addition of a two-story wing, then later the Dales further extended the house and added many luxurious features. From the entry area you pass through the kitchen to a very modern breakfast room enclosed by glass with views out to the Malvern Hills. From the entry climb the turret stairs to the dining room whose windows are set in the curvature of the turret walls. A few steps up from here is the cozy Worcester Room, whose color scheme of beiges and peach is pretty against the exposed whitewash of the timbered walls. Off the turret stair is the most popular room, the Malvern Room, with a pretty, soft-yellow pattern of fleur-de-lys and a wall of windows looking across to the Malvern Hills. Downstairs is the Stratford Room whose windows look out onto the quarry garden. Set under dark beams, the deep rose of the spread contrasts with the zebra chairs. *Directions:* Inkberrow is on the A422 between Worcester and Stratford. In the center of town, turn up Stonepit Lane, go left at the first crossroads, and the Old Windmill is the third home on the right.

THE OLD WINDMILL
Owners: Sheila & Mike Dale
Withybed Lane, Inkberrow
Worcestershire WR7 4JL, England
Tel & fax: (01386) 792801
Email: sheila@theoldwindmill.co.uk
3 rooms
£45 per person, dinner £22.50
Open all year, Credit cards: VS
Children by arrangement, No-smoking house
www.karenbrown.com/england/windmill.html

The Faulkners (thought to be a derivative of "falconers") started out as a Wealden Hall House in the 15th century. The second-floor bedrooms were incorporated some 200 years later and feature numerous exposed beams. The two single rooms share a private bathroom while the double has its own facilities and also expansive views over the grounds and garden. Home to the Rigby family and their schnauzer, Connie, the house showcases Celia's antiques and a fascinating array of collectibles: locks, hats, cane baskets, galvanized buckets, bread boards, and carved wooden decoys, to mention but a few. The house is set in 5 acres of meadowlands complete with paddock, ponds, and gardens, and guests are free to wander and relax in the tranquil surroundings. Take a seat in a sunny corner of the walled garden or curl up in front of the stove in the drawing room. Breakfast in the dining room is the only meal served. The seaside town of Brighton with its extravaganza of a Royal Pavilion and narrow, twisting lanes full of antique shops is a great attraction and the famous opera house at Glyndebourne is a 10-minute drive away. *Directions:* Heading north on the A26, approximately 4 miles north of Lewes take the turnoff signposted Isfield just after the Old Ship Inn. Follow the road into the village, make a left turn over the old railway crossing, and The Faulkners is approximately 1 mile farther, on the right-hand side at the second bend.

THE FAULKNERS   **New**
Owner: Celia Rigby
Isfield
East Sussex TN22 5XG, England
Tel: (01825) 750344, Fax: (01825) 750577
3 rooms
£28 per person
Closed Christmas & New Year, Credit cards: none
Children over 14, No-smoking house

No need to request a room with a view at Nonsuch House, for every room offers a spectacular panorama of the sheltered harbor of Dartmouth with its castle, houses tumbling down the wooded hillside to the river, and yachts tugging at their moorings. The view won the hearts of Patricia, Geoffrey, and Christopher Noble (a parents-and-son trio) who decided to reduce the workload involved in running an upscale country house hotel (Langshott Manor) and concentrate on the aspect of the hospitality business that gives them most satisfaction—looking after their guests. After a day of sightseeing, enjoy a set, three-course dinner in the conservatory and watch the activity in the harbor below. Bedrooms, which come with a choice of queen, king, or twin beds, are absolutely delightful and each is accompanied by an immaculate modern bathroom. A fun day trip involves taking a ferry and steam train into Paignton. On Tuesdays in summer you can take the ferry to Totnes and stroll around the market admiring the townsfolk in their colorful Elizabethan costumes. *Directions:* Two miles before Brixham on the A3022 take the A379. After 2 miles fork left onto the B3205 for Kingswear, go onto the one-way system through the woods, and take the first left up Higher Contour Road. Go down Ridley Hill and Nonsuch House is on the seaward side at the hairpin bend. Parking is on the street.

NONSUCH HOUSE
Owners: Patricia, Geoffrey & Kit Noble
Church Hill
Kingswear, Dartmouth
Devon TQ6 0BX, England
Tel: (01803) 752829, Fax: (01803) 752357
Email: enquiries@nonsuch-house.co.uk
5 rooms
£40 per person, dinner £21.50
Open all year, Credit cards: none
Children over 10
www.karenbrown.com/ews/nonsuch.html

Lavenham with its lovely timbered buildings, ancient guildhall, and spectacular church is the most attractive village in Suffolk. The Great House on the corner of the market square, a 15th-century building with an imposing 18th-century façade, houses a French restaurant-with-rooms run by Martine and Regis Crepy. Dinner is served in the oak-beamed dining room with candlelight and soft music and is particularly good value for money from Monday to Friday when a fixed-price menu is offered. On Saturday you dine from the à-la-carte menu. The restaurant is closed on Sundays and Mondays. In summer you can dine *al fresco* in the flower-filled courtyard. The large bedrooms all have a lounge or a sitting area and bathroom. Architecturally the rooms are divinely old-world, with sloping plank floors, creaking floorboards, little windows, and a plethora of beams. Enjoy the village in the peace and quiet of the evening after the throng of daytime summer visitors has departed. Next door, Little Hall is furnished in turn-of-the-century style and is open as a museum. Farther afield are other historic villages such as Kersey and Long Melford, and Constable's Flatford Mill. *Directions*: Lavenham is on the A1141 between Bury St. Edmunds and Hadleigh.

THE GREAT HOUSE
Owners: Martine & Regis Crepy
Market Place
Lavenham
Suffolk CO10 9QZ, England
Tel: (01787) 247431, Fax: (01787) 248007
Email: greathouse@clara.co.uk
5 rooms
£45–£70 per person, dinner £19.95 (not Sun or Mon)
Closed Jan, Credit cards: all major
Children welcome
www.karenbrown.com/ews/greathouse.html

I could spend hours sitting in Lavenham Priory's old Great Hall just soaking up the atmosphere of this impressive Elizabethan merchant's home, which began life in the 13th century as a Benedictine priory. It's an absolutely superb room with its stone-flagged floor, huge sofas drawn round the massive stone fireplace, and beams patterning the simple white walls rising to the rafters. Bedrooms enjoy the same airy spaciousness and are furnished to utter perfection. Whether you choose the Great Chamber with its ornately draped bed; the Painted Chamber with its four-poster bed and Elizabethan wall paintings; or the snugger quarters of the twin-bedded Garden Chamber, you will be completely charmed by your room. Breakfast is the only meal served but there is no shortage of places to walk to for dinner. Because of the popularity of this exceptional home it is advisable to make reservations well in advance. Lavenham, in Tudor times one of England's wealthiest towns, is now a picturesque village with leaning timbered houses lining its streets and continuing into its market square where the Guildhall presents displays of local history and the medieval wool industry. *Directions:* Arriving in Lavenham, turn down the side of The Swan into Water Street, then go right after 50 yards into the private drive and Priory's car park.

LAVENHAM PRIORY
Owners: Gilli & Tim Pitt
Water Street
Lavenham
Suffolk CO10 9RW, England
Tel: (01787) 247404, Fax: (01787) 284472
Email: mail@lavenhampriory.co.uk
5 rooms
£39–£54 per person
Closed Christmas & New Year, Credit cards: MC, VS
Children over 10, No-smoking house
www.karenbrown.com/england/priory.html

I certainly saved the best for last on my 2001 research trip: a visit to Angela and Hugh Jefferson at Hallend, an exquisitely decorated, quintessentially Georgian country house set in several acres of gardens and equestrian estate. Angela has made extensive use of designer fabrics, with antiques, collectibles, and artwork completing the picture. Two tastefully decorated double rooms with enviable en-suite bathrooms are available in the main house. The front bedroom is the larger and features a luxurious modern bathroom with double washbasins and separate shower and tub. The bathroom for the equally lovely but slightly smaller four-poster room is equipped with a shower. Sometimes, for families traveling together, an additional four-poster room is available with this room. Guests have full run of the house—drawing room, TV room, library, and formal dining room. Breakfast is served on a large circular table in the breakfast room off the designer kitchen, which is worth a visit in its own right. On warm days guests eat breakfast in the conservatory or on the patio next to the outdoor pool. Across the courtyard there is a self-contained, fully equipped, one-bedroom cottage. *Directions:* From Ledbury take the A449 west to Preston Cross roundabout. Turn right towards Leominster on the A4172. After 1 mile turn left for Aylton, continue for 1¼ miles to the T-junction then turn left (signposted Fuchsia Collection). Go past the Fuchsia Collection to a T-junction and Hallend is straight in front of you. Go left and turn into the first drive on the right.

*HALLEND   **New***
Owners: Angela & Hugh Jefferson
Kynaston, Ledbury
Herefordshire HR8 2PD, England
Tel: (01531) 670225, Fax: (01531) 670747
Email: khjefferson@hallend91.freeserve.co.uk
2 rooms, 1 cottage
£37.50–£50 per person
Closed Christmas, Credit cards: MC, VS
Children over 12, No-smoking house
www.karenbrown.com/england/hallend.html

Buckton is a cluster of cottages and a couple of farms lining a quiet country lane on the outskirts of the pretty village of Leintwardine in the heart of the Marches, once an area of much inter-fiefdom feuding and armed conflict along the Welsh border. A 12th-century motte (mound) from a motte and bailey castle sits at the bottom of Yvonne and Hayden Lloyd's garden as evidence of the area's turbulent history. The substantial, tall Georgian farmhouse, very typical of those in this area, is a working farm with Hayden raising cattle and sheep and growing cereal. Three attractive bedrooms are found up the steep, broad flight of stairs. The double-bedded room has an en-suite shower room while the two twin-bedded rooms have their own private bathrooms across the hall. The Lloyds have an easy, welcoming way with guests that makes them feel very much a part of the family. Visiting castles is a popular pastime and they come in all shapes and sizes, from tiny Stokesay to grand Powys. Yvonne plans a route for guests through the unspoiled black-and-white timbered villages of neighboring Herefordshire. *Directions:* From Ludlow take the A49 north towards Shrewsbury for 3 miles and turn left on the A4113 towards Knighton. Cross the bridge in Leintwardine and take the first right (still A4113) to Walford (1 mile) where you turn right for Buckton. Follow the narrow lane and Upper Buckton is the second farm on the left.

UPPER BUCKTON
Owners: Yvonne & Hayden Lloyd
Upper Buckton
Leintwardine, near Craven Arms
Shropshire SY7 0JU, England
Tel & fax: (01547) 540634
3 rooms
£30–£35 per person, dinner £20
Open all year, Credit cards: none
Children welcome, No-smoking house

Springfield House, with its sweep of lawn down to the meandering River Granta, is the most comfortable of family homes sitting behind a prim, early-Victorian exterior. It's an exceptionally quiet little spot just steps from the heart of this peaceful Cambridgeshire village. Judith offers a warm welcome to her home where guests have their own sitting and dining rooms, both overlooking the garden and the river. On warm summer mornings breakfast—the only meal offered—is often served in the conservatory. Judith has several bedrooms with different-sized bed and bathroom combinations so that she can accommodate all preferences. I particularly liked her front bedroom where a high queen bed gives you a super view of the garden. (The bed, like husband Fred, hails from America.) Fred, a total Anglophile, has a distinguished American heritage, with an ancestor who served as an aide-de-camp to George Washington. Another lovely bedroom has its own private staircase and overlooks the courtyard. Cambridge lies 10 miles away and Judith points you in the right direction on what to see and do there. There are many picturesque towns and villages within easy reach such as Thaxted, renowned for its beautiful church, Clare and Long Melford, noted for their antique shops, and Lavenham, famous for its Guildhall. *Directions:* From Cambridge take the A1307 towards Haverhill for 10 miles to Linton. Turn left into High Street and first right after The Crown (on the left) into Horn Lane. Springfield House is on the right just beyond the chapel.

SPRINGFIELD HOUSE
Owners: Judith & Fred Rossiter
14–16 Horn Lane
Linton
Cambridgeshire CB1 6HT, England
Tel: (01223) 891383, Fax: (01223) 890335
3 rooms
£25–£27.50 per person
Open all year, Credit cards: none
Children welcome, No-smoking house

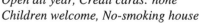

Tucked in an unspoilt valley high above the hustle and bustle of the more well-known Lake District tourist routes, this traditional pub lies surrounded by the ruggedly beautiful Lakeland scenery. Built of somber-looking slate in 1872 as a resting place for travelers, the hostelry is still a base for tourists, many of whom come here for the walking. They gather by the bar, the sound of their hiking boots echoing hollowly against the slate floor, poring over maps and discussing the day's activities. By contrast, the carpeted and curtained dining room and lounge with its velour chairs seem very sedate. The Stephenson family pride themselves on the quality of their food and offer a five-course meal in addition to substantial bar meals. Recently refurbished bedrooms maintain the character of a 19th-century inn. For travelers who enjoy prettily decorated, simply furnished, and spotlessly clean rooms with modern bathrooms, the Three Shires fits the bill. Just a few miles away are some of the Lake District's most popular villages: Hawkshead, Ambleside, Coniston, and Grasmere. *Directions:* From Ambleside take the A593, Coniston road, cross Skelwith Bridge, and take the first right, signposted The Langdales and Wrynose Pass. Take the first left to Little Langdale and the Three Shires Inn is on your right.

THREE SHIRES INN
Owners: Stephenson family
Little Langdale
Ambleside
Cumbria LA22 9NZ, England
Tel: (015394) 37215, Fax: (015394) 37127
Email: ian@threeshiresinn.com
10 rooms
£29.50–£43 per person, dinner £20
Closed Jan, Credit cards: MC, VS
Children welcome
www.karenbrown.com/england/threeshiresinn.html

From the front, Wood Hall appears to be a substantial, classic Georgian home, but step round the back and you discover beams and plasterwork, for the Georgian frontage is a façade placed on a 1480 Tudor home. A Victorian owner made his contribution to the house in the 1840s when he added tall windows that flood the entire house with light. This blend of architectural periods gives Susan and Patrick Nisbett's home great charm. While Patrick has the interesting occupation of designing church vestments, Susan takes care of her guests, the family, and the pets. The house is large enough to give guests their own "end" of the house where a vast dining room with a polished table sitting center stage and armchairs in the tall bay window doubles as a guests' breakfast and sitting room. A broad staircase leads up to the bedrooms. The very pretty queen-bedded room has a shower, while the lovely twin-bedded room has a bathroom. Both are large enough to accommodate seating areas where you can relax or watch TV. With advanced notice Susan may provide dinner though you'll find that there is no shortage of excellent eating places nearby, among them The Swan at Monks Eleigh or The White Rose at Lindsey. Just up the road lies Lavenham with its many leaning timbered houses. *Directions:* Take the B115 from Sudbury towards Lavenham for 3½ miles. Turn right to Little Waldingfield and the house is on the left 200 yards beyond The Swan pub.

WOOD HALL
Owners: Susan & Patrick Nisbett
Little Waldingfield
Suffolk CO10 0SY, England
Tel: (01787) 247362, Fax: (01787) 248326
Email: nisbett@nisbett.enta.net
2 rooms
£32.50–£35 per person, dinner £15 (not Sun)
Closed Christmas, Credit cards: none
Children over 12
www.karenbrown.com/england/woodhall.html

Built in 1673 as a rectory, Landewednack House sits above the 6th-century church and a cluster of cottages that lead down to the rocky inlet of Church Cove at the tip of the Lizard Peninsula, the southernmost spot in England. Restored to a state of luxury unknown to former residents, Landewednack House was purchased by Marion and Peter Stanley who fell in love with the house, its walled garden, and magnificent views. Guests are welcomed with a traditional Cornish tea of scones, clotted cream, and strawberry jam served in the elegant sitting room, secluded garden, or by the sheltered swimming pool. In the evening guests may dine together in the dining room before a log fire in the massive 17th-century fireplace or separately in the beamed morning room. The starched linen coverlets on the polished mahogany half-tester bed in the Yellow Room present a dramatic picture in a room whose floor-to-ceiling bay window frames a lovely view of the garden and the church silhouetted against the sea. Choose the Red Room for its 18th-century four-poster bed or the Chinese Room for its silk-draped king-sized bed that can also be twins. Walk along the clifftops to the adorable village of Cadgwith or visit the many beautiful Cornish gardens close by. *Directions:* From Helston, take the A3083 to Lizard (do *not* turn right at the first Church Cove sign near Helston). Turn left before entering the village, signposted Church Cove. Take the next left (Church Cove and Lifeboat Station) and Landewednack is on the left.

LANDEWEDNACK HOUSE
Owners: Marion & Peter Stanley
Church Cove, Lizard, Helston
Cornwall TR12 7PQ, England
Tel: (01326) 290909, Fax: (01326) 290192
Email: landewednack.house@virgin.net
3 rooms
£40–£48 per person, dinner from £22.95
Closed Christmas, Credit cards: MC, VS
Children over 16, No-smoking house
www.karenbrown.com/england/landewednack.html

The Virginia-creeper-clad Fox Inn, dating back to the 16th century, is a classic small English pub, replete with flagstone floors, beams, and fireplaces, situated in the heart of the Cotswolds. Three newly renovated and tastefully decorated double bedrooms await upstairs, each with its own resident fox nestled on the pillow to greet you. Two have bathrooms en suite, while the other has its own private facilities. All provide inviting havens to lay your head at the end of a long day of touring—but not before sampling the award-winning epicurean delights downstairs in the Red Room with its welcoming fireplace and walls adorned with a fascinating display of antique corkscrews and bottle- and wine-related memorabilia. Meals can also be served in the bar or outside on the patio where a new hi-tech retractable awning equipped with lights and space heaters helps to offset the vagaries of the English summer weather. An extensive and reasonably priced menu is complemented by a comprehensive, value-packed wine list. Lovely Cotswold villages to explore include Chipping Campden, Bourton-on-the-Water, Upper and Lower Slaughter, Stow-on-the-Wold, Bibury, and Broadway. Garden lovers will enjoy Kiftsgate, Hidcote Manor, and Batsford. *Directions:* Travel north on the A429 into Stow-on-the-Wold and turn right on the A436 towards Chipping Norton. Proceed downhill for 3 miles. After passing a garage on the right-hand side, take the second right to Lower Oddington. The Fox is easily found in the center of the village.

THE FOX INN   New
Owners: Sally & Kirk Ritchie
Lower Oddington, near Stow-on-the-Wold
Gloucestershire GL56 OUR, England
Tel: (01451) 870555, Fax: (01451) 870669
Email: info@foxinn.net
3 rooms
£29–£42.50 per person*, dinner £17.50
*Continental breakfast only
Open all year, Credit cards: MC, VS
Children welcome
www.karenbrown.com/england/foxinnoddington.html

Originally a monastery with cellars dating back to the 14th century, this house was confiscated from a past owner by Henry VIII. More recently a working farmhouse, it has now been purchased and renovated by owners Sybil and Robert Gisby, no newcomers to the bed and breakfast business. Upstairs are three spacious bedrooms, each with its own thoroughly modern and luxurious bathroom en suite, as well as expansive views across the surrounding countryside. My particular favorite features an enormous crimson soaking tub. Downstairs, guests can relax in the sitting room with its comfortable sofas, inglenook fireplace equipped with wood-burning stove, and a plentiful supply of reading matter. A window seat provides views of the front garden. Breakfast is served farmhouse-style in the kitchen or in the conservatory, which is shaded by an impressive Black Hamburg grapevine or, weather permitting, outside on the patio next to the decorative fishpond. Lower and Upper Swell date back to Roman times, as evidenced by the coins found when Lower Swell's church was being restored. Exploring Cotswold villages is a popular pastime, with Bourton-on-the-Water, Stow-on-the-Wold, Chipping Campden, and Broadway being popular destinations. *Directions:* From the A429 at Stow-on-the-Wold take the B4068 signposted to Lower Swell. Turn left into a private driveway just before the Golden Globe Inn.

RECTORY FARMHOUSE   New
Owners: Sybil & Robert Gisby
Lower Swell, near Stow-on-the-Wold
Cheltenham, Gloucestershire GL54 1LH, England
Tel: (01451) 832351, Fax: none
Email: rectory.farmhouse@cw-warwick.co.uk
3 rooms
£35–£40 per person
Closed Christmas & New Year, Credit cards: none
Children 16 & over, No-smoking house
www.karenbrown.com/england/rectoryfarmhouse.html

This endearing cottage dates back to the early 14th century when it was home to a yeoman farmer. With its little upstairs windows peeking out from beneath a heavy thatched roof and its timber-framed wall fronted by a flower-filled garden, Loxley Farm presents an idyllic picture. The picture-book ambiance is continued inside where guests breakfast together round a long table in the low-beamed dining room. Accommodation is across the garden in the converted 17th-century thatched, half-timbered cart barn with two modern, functional suites. The Hayloft Suite has vaulted ceilings, bedroom, bathroom, sitting room, and small kitchen, while the more desirable Garden Suite has bedroom, bathroom, and garden room whose semi-circular glass walls look over the orchard, lawns, and house. Breakfast is the only meal served in the farmhouse dining room and guests often walk into Loxley or go to The Bell in Alderminster for dinner. A quiet back road brings you into the center of Stratford-upon-Avon (4 miles) with its historical timbered buildings, lovely shops, and Royal Shakespeare Theatre. In nearby Shottery is Anne Hathaway's picture-book cottage. Warwick Castle and Coventry Cathedral are both easily visited from Loxley. *Directions:* Loxley is signposted off the A422 Stratford-upon-Avon to Banbury road about 4 miles from Stratford on the left. Go through the village to the bottom of the hill, turn left (Stratford-upon-Avon), and Loxley Farm is the third house on the right.

LOXLEY FARM
Owners: Anne & Rod Horton
Loxley
Warwickshire CV35 9JN, England
Tel: (01789) 840265, Fax: (01789) 840645
2 rooms
£30–£33 per person
Closed Dec, Credit cards: none
Children welcome
www.karenbrown.com/england/loxleyfarm.html

Set in 12 acres of pasture on an upper reach of the River Avon, The Old Rectory dates back to the 14th century. It is now home to the Eldred family and their assortment of dogs, cats, and horses. The house is surrounded by its gardens (which provide flowers and seasonal produce for the house) and orchard. Two ample bedrooms with en-suite bathrooms are elegantly furnished with pretty fabrics, antiques, and pictures. An open fire warms the drawing room on cooler days, while the tennis court and heated swimming pool beckon in summer. Breakfast is served in the dining room. Nearby Bath and Malmesbury provide a wide range of possibilities for lunch and dinner. Don't miss out on a short visit to the village church, accessible though a gate in the garden wall. There are many places of interest round and about: Blenheim Palace (home of the Churchills, including the great soldier, the Duke of Marlborough); Oxford (with its colleges and punting on the river); Bath (famous for its Romans baths and Georgian architecture); and the Cotswold villages. *Directions:* Leave the M4 at junction 17 and head north following signs to Malmesbury, Sherston, and Luckington. The Old Rectory is on the left about ¼ mile before the village.

THE OLD RECTORY   New
Owners: Maril & John Eldred
Luckington, near Chippenham
Wiltshire SN14 6PQ, England
Tel: (01666) 840556, Fax: (01666) 840989
Email: b&b@the-eldreds.co.uk
2 rooms
£35 per person
Closed Christmas, Credit cards: none
Children welcome, No-smoking house
www.karenbrown.com/england/oldrectoryluckington.html

Set in a sheltered valley in the center of Exmoor National Park, this farm complex encompasses several 14th-century barns and a 200-year-old farmhouse set round a cobbled courtyard. Hens, guinea fowl, and peacocks complete the idyllic countryside picture. Three very nice bedrooms are found in the sturdy farmhouse: the attractive twin-bedded room is my favorite because of its spaciousness, airy decor, two comfortable armchairs, and lovely countryside views. The same view is shared by the adjacent four-poster room, while a small double-bedded room is found at the back of the house. If you are traveling with younger children, you might want to stay on a bed-and-breakfast basis in one of the self-catering cottages in the ancient barns. Ann provides a set three-course candlelit dinner and guests are welcome to bring their own wine to accompany their meal. Guests can fish in the Durbins' trout lake or go salmon-fishing on the nearby Exe and Barle rivers. Exmoor has delightful little unspoilt villages nestling in wooded valleys, rugged moorlands where sheep and ponies graze, and a coastline with the delightful seaside towns of Lynton and Lynmouth and the quaint little village of Porlock Weir. *Directions:* Exit the M5 at junction 25, take the A358 (Minehead road) for 5 miles, bypassing Bishops Lydeard, and turn left on the B3224 to Wheddon Cross. Go straight across the main street of the village and Cutthorne is on your left after 3 miles.

CUTTHORNE
Owners: Ann & Philip Durbin
Luckwell Bridge, Wheddon Cross
Somerset TA24 7EW, England
Tel & fax: (01643) 831255
Email: durbin@cutthorne.co.uk
3 rooms, 2 cottages
£25–£31 per person, dinner £15
Open all year, Credit cards: none
Children over 12 in house, any age in cottages
No-smoking house
www.karenbrown.com/england/cutthorne.html

The Salweys of Shropshire can trace their lineage hereabouts back to 1216 and The Lodge has been in their family since it was built in the early 1700s, but it is definitely not a formal place. Hermione puts guests at ease, encouraging them to feel as though they are friends of the family, and enjoys pointing out the architectural details of the house and explaining who's who amongst the family portraits. In the evening, guests gather in the morning room and help themselves to drinks from the honesty bar before going into dinner at a spectacular long table made of burled wood, made especially for the house. Up the grand staircase the three large bedrooms are most attractive: Chinese has a suite of furniture painted in an Asian motif, Roses is a large double with an enormous bathroom, and The Yellow Room is a large twin with its bathroom across the hall. The large garden, woodland, and farmland make this an ideal place for walking. The nearest tourist attraction is the medieval town of Ludlow with its old inns, alleyways of antique shops, Norman castle, and riverside walks. *Directions:* Leave Ludlow over Ludford Bridge traveling south. After 1½ miles turn right on the B4361 signposted Richards Castle. After 400 yards turn right through the entrance gates of The Lodge by a curved stone wall, and continue up the long drive to the house.

THE LODGE
Owners: Hermione & Humphrey Salwey
Ludlow
Shropshire SY8 4DU, England
Tel: (01584) 872103, Fax: (01584) 876126
3 rooms
£40 per person, dinner £20 (wine included)
Open Apr to Oct, Credit cards: none
Children not accepted, No-smoking house

Ludlow is a charming town of cobblestone streets rising from the River Teme to its Norman castle. The most delightful street in town is Lower Broad Street, which narrows to Broadgate, the 13th-century gatehouse. The architecture of Lower Broad Street runs the gamut from Tudor through Georgian to Victorian and Number Twenty Eight offers you accommodation in houses of each style. My favorite place to stay is Bromley Court where three adorable tiny Tudor cottages combine to form a secluded haven round a small walled garden. Each cottage has a beamed sitting room, adorable bedroom, top-of-the-line bathroom, and breakfast bar with refrigerator stocked with breakfast goodies. Number Twenty Eight itself is Georgian. You step directly from the street into a cozy parlor with an open fire, book-lined walls, prints, plates, and pictures, and a warm welcome from Patricia and Philip Ross. Most guests congregate here for breakfast, which in summer is served on the flower-filled terrace. Broadgate Mews is Tudor, with two bedrooms and a sitting room, while the delightful Westview is a restored Victorian terrace home offering especially nice bedrooms with brass-and-wrought-iron beds and spacious, very up-to-date bathrooms. Dine in one of Ludlow's fine restaurants, explore the immense Norman castle, and wander the lanes with their many book and antique shops. *Directions:* From the south, fork left off the A49 onto the B4361 signposted Ludlow south and Richards Castle. Cross the river and go straight into Lower Broad Street.

NUMBER TWENTY EIGHT
Owners: Patricia & Philip Ross
Lower Broad Street
Ludlow, Shropshire SY8 1PQ, England
Tel: (01584) 876996, Fax: (01584) 876860
Reservations: (0800) 081 5000
Email: ross@no28.co.uk
6 rooms, £37.50–£45 per person
Open all year, Credit cards: MC, VS
Children welcome, No-smoking house
www.karenbrown.com/england/numbertwentyeight.html

How unusual to find an Elizabethan manor amidst the suburbs and how lucky that this manor is a 15-minute drive from Heathrow airport, making it absolutely perfect for a few nights at the beginning or end of your stay in England if you are visiting from overseas. Carved faces by the massive front door, bowed lead windows, paneling, and beams make this the most impressive of homes. Relax in the oak-paneled sitting room or curl up in the upstairs hallways nook with a cup of tea. Bedrooms are very attractive: a small double has an en-suite bathroom and a little sitting area overlooking the peaceful garden, a spacious twin is decorated in sunny yellows and has its bathroom across the hall, and my favorite, the large paneled double room, has a spacious shower room. Guests often walk to the pub down the road for dinner. Maidenhead railway station is only a mile away and a 30-minute train ride finds you in London—ideal for the theater or sightseeing. Windsor, Henley on Thames, and Marlow are a 15-minute drive away, while Oxford is 45 minutes away. *Directions:* Leave the M4 at junction 8/9 and take the A404 (M) to junction 9A signposted Cox Green. Follow the Cox Green signs at both mini-roundabouts into Cox Green Road. Turn left at the Foresters Pub and Beehive Manor is on your right in 600 yards.

BEEHIVE MANOR
Owners: Lesley & Stanley Goldstein
Cox Green Lane
Maidenhead
Berkshire SL6 3ET, England
Tel: (01628) 620980, Fax (01628) 621840
Email: beehivemanor@cs.com
3 rooms
£35 per person
Closed Christmas & New Year, Credit cards: MC, VS
Children over 10, No-smoking house
www.karenbrown.com/england/beehive.html

Conjecture has it that Thomas Hardy used Old Lamb House (then the Lamb Inn) as Rollivers Tavern in *Tess of the d'Urbervilles*. Jenny and Ben continue the tradition of hospitality by offering accommodation to guests in two large front bedrooms that share a bathroom. Guests use the front door (family members use the kitchen door) and atop the curving staircase there's a sitting area with two armchairs and lots of tourist information. Bedrooms, spacious enough to spread out in and relax, both contain comfortable, old-fashioned armchairs, TV, and tea- and coffee-making facilities. The Pink Room is decked out in soft pinks with matching flowery bedlinen and drapes, while the Blue Room is outfitted in soft blues and offers lovely views of the garden with its stately cedar tree. We thoroughly enjoyed our dinner at The Crown pub just down the road and Jenny told me that The White Horse also serves good food. Dorset abounds in country lanes that lead to pretty villages such as Milton Abbas and Cerne Abbas with its club-wielding giant carved into the chalk hillside. Shaftesbury has many steep roads running down into Blackmore Vale, the most famous being cobbled Gold Hill. *Directions:* From Shaftesbury take the A30 towards Exeter for 4 miles to East Stour. Turn left on B3092 to Marnhull (3 miles) and go half a mile beyond Marnhull church where you turn right at the triangle of grass with a signpost and into Old Lamb House's driveway.

OLD LAMB HOUSE
Owners: Jenny & Ben Chilcott
Marnhull
Dorset DT10 1QG, England
Tel: (01258) 820491, Fax: (01258) 821464
Email: ben@bcaviation.demon.co.uk
2 rooms
£25 per person
Closed Christmas & New Year, Credit cards: none
Children welcome, No-smoking house
www.karenbrown.com/england/oldlambhouse.html

Just five minutes off the A1, a country lane leads to this beautiful Georgian farmhouse, home to Eleanor and John Harrop for over 20 years. In fact, the farm is much older but it was extensively remodeled in 1790 when three little cottages were combined into the farmhouse. The Harrops operate on the ethos of treating guests like visiting friends. They are experienced and welcoming hosts and guests can have as much or as little family togetherness as they like. There are no televisions or phones and because of the countryside location you have utter peace and quiet. Upstairs, two spacious bedrooms, one twin-bedded, one double, have their large private bathrooms across the landing. Make yourself at home in the drawing room, read, plan your excursions into North Yorkshire, and chat with Eleanor as she prepares your breakfast in the kitchen. For dinner there are country pubs and restaurants within a short drive and there may be the possibility of eating dinner-party-style with your hosts in the formal dining room. It's an ideal place to stop off on the journey to or from Scotland but it would be a shame to come to this lovely part of the country without taking in a few castles (Richmond, Middleham, Barnard, Raby), cathedrals (Durham, Ripon, York), gardens, and houses (Newby, Bowes, Rokeby). *Directions:* Leave the A1 at Scotch Corner (A66 junction) and go to Middleton Tyas. Take the Croft road for 1 mile and turn right at a sharp bend. Brook House is the first house down the lane.

BROOK HOUSE
Owners: Eleanor & John Harrop
Middleton Tyas, Richmond
North Yorkshire DL10 6RP, England
Tel & fax: (01325) 377713
2 rooms
£35 per person, dinner £23
Closed Christmas & New Year, Credit cards: none
Children over 16

We heard about Jörgen Kunath and Anthony Ma's Old Vicarage from a reader who had had a thoroughly enjoyable time there and raved about the delectable food. That is what led us to this handsome Victorian house on the edge of the charming Dorset village of Milborne Port. They simply do not build homes on this scale any more—bedrooms in the house are oh-so-spacious and the sitting room vast. If you prefer snugger rooms, opt for those in the adjacent coach house. All are decorated with great flair, with antiques and Oriental works of art combined in a colorful and altogether satisfying way. The same attention to detail found in the guestrooms is also found in the excellent cooking. Anthony, who for many years ran an acclaimed London restaurant with Jörgen, serves an indulgent breakfast and on Friday and Saturday nights produces dinners that incorporate a unique blend of traditional and innovative cuisine. There are enough things to do in the area to keep you here for a week. Just to the north lie the magnificent grounds of Stourhead and the picturesque market town of Castle Cary. Meander south to the coast through idyllic Dorset villages including Cerne Abbas (be sure to see the giant), Kingston Lacy, and Milton Abbas to the coast. Going west you come to Montecute House where *Sense and Sensibility* was filmed and Parnham House, famous for its furniture design. *Directions:* From Sherborne take the A30 towards Shaftesbury for 2 miles to Milborne Port where you find The Old Vicarage on the right.

THE OLD VICARAGE
Owners: Jörgen Kunath & Anthony Ma
Sherborne Road
Milborne Port
Dorset DT9 5AT, England
Tel: (01963) 251117, Fax: (01963) 251515
Email: theoldvicarage@milborneport.freeserve.co.uk
7 rooms
£30.50–£39 per person, Dinner £22.90 (Fri & Sat)
Closed Jan, Credit cards: all major
Children over 5
www.karenbrown.com/england/milborneport.html

Neighbrook is a handsome stone manor house in 36 acres of grounds, the elegant country home of the Playfair family who welcome their guests most warmly. Guests enter off the back graveled courtyard through a door distinguished by a brass, mustached sun into a stone-floor entry area. The guest salon is beautiful. A grouping of rose-colored sofas is set around a large open fireplace and large windows look out on two sides to the front lawn and gardens. Guestrooms are found up a back staircase. The front corner room has a double bed and en-suite bathroom with a marvelous old pine tub, soft pink-and-blue floral fabric, and gorgeous views. A cozy single room with washbasin shares a bath at the end of the hall with the Playfair children (when they are in residence—and guests are favored with first use!). Up more stairs you find a handsome double-bedded room with steps up to a spacious sitting room containing two more single beds and a bathroom looking out to the back. Dining with the Playfairs (by arrangement) is a special treat. Their dining room is elegant: one long trestle table runs the length of the room encircled by handsome windows curtained in colors of soft yellow, cream, and green. *Directions:* Travel north from Moreton in Marsh for 3 miles on the A429 towards Stratford. Turn west on the road signed Aston Magna then right on the road just in front of the village's first building and travel a short distance to the entry gates of Neighbrook Manor.

NEIGHBROOK MANOR
Owners: Camilla & John Playfair
Aston Magna
Moreton in Marsh
Gloucestershire GL56 9QP, England
Tel: (01386) 593232, Fax: (01386) 593500
Email: info@neighbrookmanor.com
3 rooms
£38 per person, dinner £24
Closed Christmas, Credit cards: MC, VS
Children welcome
www.karenbrown.com/england/neighbrook.html

Mungrisdale is one of the few unspoilt villages left in the Lake District and is made up of a pub, an old church, and a cluster of houses and farms set at the foot of rugged, gray-blue crags. Do not confuse The Mill with the adjoining pub, The Mill Inn: drive through the car park of the inn to reach private parking for this cozy hotel. Rooms are of cottage proportions: a small lounge with comfy chairs gathered round a blazing log fire, a cozy dining room where each small oak table is set with blue napkins, candles, willow-pattern china, and a tiny flower arrangement, and nine small bedrooms with matching draperies and bedspreads. Most visitors are drawn here for the dinners prepared by Eleanor. Dinner consists of an appetizer followed by a tasty homemade soup served with soda bread (the latter a popular fixture on the menu), a main course (with a vegetarian alternative), dessert, and cheese and biscuits. Bookings for bed and breakfast only are not usually accepted. The Lake District is a beautiful region, popular with walkers and sightseers alike. Some of its premier villages are Coniston, Hawkshead, Sawrey (home of Beatrix Potter), Ambleside, and Grasmere. *Directions:* Leave the M6 at junction 40 and take the A66 towards Keswick for 10 miles. The Mill is 2 miles north of this road and the signpost for Mungrisdale is midway between Penrith and Keswick.

THE MILL HOTEL
Owners: Eleanor & Richard Quinlan
Mungrisdale
Penrith
Cumbria CA11 0XR, England
Tel: (017687) 79659, Fax: (017687) 79155
9 rooms
£59–£75 per person dinner, B&B
Open Mar to Nov, Credit cards: none
Children welcome
www.karenbrown.com/england/themillhotel.html

In her younger years Beatrix Potter used to visit Ees Wyke House with her family. Now it is a very pleasant hotel run by Mag and John Williams who have painted and decorated the house from top to bottom in a comfortable style. John, a former cookery teacher at a catering college, enjoys cooking and his dinner menu always offers choices of starter, main course, and dessert. Dinner is taken in the large dining room with glorious views across the countryside. The bedrooms have tall windows framing gorgeous countryside views and many overlook nearby Esthwaite Water. Tucked under the eaves, two airy, spacious attic bedrooms have super views: one has a bathroom en suite while the other has a private bath just next door. The other bedrooms also have a mix of en-suite and adjacent bathroom arrangements. The smallest bedroom, on the ground floor, is reserved for visitors who have difficulty with stairs but unfortunately has no view. A short stroll up the village brings you to Hill Top Farm where Beatrix Potter wrote several of her books. Walks abound in the area and the more oft-trod Lakeland routes are easily accessible by taking the nearby ferry across Lake Windermere. *Directions:* From Ambleside take the A593 towards Coniston. After about a mile turn left on the B5286 to Hawkshead. Skirt Hawkshead village and follow signs for the ferry. Ees Wyke House is on the right just before Sawrey.

EES WYKE COUNTRY HOUSE HOTEL
Owners: Mag & John Williams
Near Sawrey
Hawkshead, Ambleside
Cumbria LA22 0JZ, England
Tel & fax: (015394) 36393
8 rooms
£48–£50 per person, dinner £15
Open Mar to Dec, Credit cards: AX
Children over 10

This historic and lovely country house dating from 1830 and enlarged in the 20th century might now be an abandoned ruin but for the courage and hard work of Shirley and Colin Whiteside, former bankers. They spotted the place while on a walking holiday and bought it on the spur of the moment. This led to a great deal of hard work, which has resulted in this solid Victorian home being returned to its former glory. The house is comfortably furnished and has a relaxing feel to it. The back terrace looks across the terraced gardens to the distant hills while the spacious dining room offers views across the gardens to Esthwaite Water and the Grizdale Forest. Bedrooms are very comfortable: two are on the ground floor and the rest distributed between the top two floors. The higher you climb, the more spectacular the view. Because of the immense popularity of this village, with Beatrix Potter's Hill Top Farm just up the road, Sawrey House (by prior arrangement) occasionally accepts coach parties for lunch. Staying here gives you not only close access to Beatrix's first Lake District home but also the chance to wander the lanes and fields that she included in her famous stories. The ferry to Windermere is just 2 miles away, making the Lake District easily accessible for touring by car. *Directions:* From Ambleside take the A593 towards Coniston. After about a mile turn left on the B5286 to Hawkshead. Skirt Hawkshead village and follow signs for the ferry. Sawrey House is on the right just before Sawrey.

SAWREY HOUSE
Owners: Shirley & Colin Whiteside
Near Sawrey, Ambleside
Cumbria LA22 OLF, England
Tel: (015394) 36387, Fax: (015394) 36010
11 rooms
£45–£56 per person, dinner £20
Closed Nov & Jan, Credit cards: MC, VS
Children over 8

The quiet, narrow country lane that runs in front of Fosse Farmhouse is the historical Fosse Way, the road built by the Romans to connect their most important forts from Devon to Lincolnshire. Inside, Caron Cooper has furnished her rooms with great flair, using soft colors and enviable country-French antiques in every room. Charming knickknacks and country china adorn much of the sitting and breakfast rooms and most pieces are for sale. Upstairs, there are three extremely comfortable guest bedrooms. My favorite was the Pine Room with its mellow pine furniture and especially spacious, luxuriously equipped bathroom. With advance notice, Caron enjoys preparing an imaginative, three-course dinner, and is happy to cater to vegetarian palates. At Christmas Caron offers a three-day festive holiday. This tranquil countryside setting is within an easy half-hour's drive of Bath, Bristol, Tetbury, and Cirencester, and the picture-perfect village of Castle Combe is also nearby. *Directions:* Exit the M4 at junction 17 towards Chippenham, turn right on the A420 (Bristol road) for 3 miles to the B4039, which you take around Castle Combe to The Gib where you turn left opposite The Salutation Inn. Fosse Farmhouse is on your right after 1 mile.

FOSSE FARMHOUSE
Owner: Caron Cooper
Nettleton Shrub
Nettleton, Chippenham
Wiltshire SN14 7NJ, England
Tel: (01249) 782286, Fax: (01249) 783066
Email: caroncooper@compuserve.com
3 rooms
£55–£65 per person, dinner £25
Open all year, Credit cards: all major
Children welcome
www.karenbrown.com/england/fossefarmhouse.html

Sitting at the head of Wensleydale, Newton le Willows is a very quiet village off the beaten track—a cluster of houses, a pub, and The Hall, home to Oriella Featherstone. Oriella is just as flamboyant as her name suggests and her house is decorated like herself, in a graciously extravagant manner. Artfully draped curtains cascading to the floors hang from all the windows and many of the doors. Sofas are piled with plump cushions, plants trail from pots, and grand flower arrangements grace lovely pieces of furniture, while the dining table is set in the evening with silver service enhanced by twinkling candlelight. Relax in the comfortable drawing room or curl up by the fire in the intimate snug. Oriella has five bedrooms though she never takes more than six guests. All are decorated lavishly and vary in size from spacious to grand (the suite that spans the house). Nearby eating places offer food ranging from inexpensive to some of the best in Britain. Within a half-hour's drive of this lovely part of Yorkshire are Middleham with its racing stables and ruined castle of Richard II, Bolton Castle where Mary, Queen of Scots was held captive, and the ruins of Jervaulx and Fountains abbeys. *Directions:* Leave the A1 at Leeming Bar taking the A684 to Bedale. At the main street turn right and half a mile out of town take the first left, signposted Newton le Willows. Continue to the T-junction and turn right. At the Wheatsheaf Inn turn left and right into The Hall's driveway.

THE HALL
Owner: Oriella Featherstone
Newton le Willows
Near Bedale
Yorkshire DL8 1SW, England
Tel: (01677) 450210, Fax: (01677) 450014
5 rooms
£45–£50 per person, dinner £25
Open all year, Credit cards: none
Children over 13

This 17th-century former woolen mill deep in the heart of the Devon countryside is now the most welcoming of casual country hotels run with great style by Hazel Phillips and Peter Hunt. It's an informal spot where Peter greets you in the flagstoned hallway and shows you up to your room, encouraging you to make yourself thoroughly at home. After a drink in the bar when Peter passes out the menus, with three choices for each of the three courses, you are shown into the little dining room with its pine tables and chairs set before a massive inglenook fireplace (dinner with reservations Tuesday to Saturday). Upstairs all but one of the simply decorated, cozy bedrooms have snug bathrooms or showers en suite. Peter is an avid beekeeper and after sampling his honey for breakfast, guests often purchase a pot to enjoy back home. Peter's other great interest is his flock of Jacob sheep—woolen garments "fresh from the flock" are often for sale. It's a tremendous place to relax and unwind: sit on the lawn and listen to the burble of the River Bovey flowing alongside, or walk along the river and up on the moors. Birdwatching is a great attraction here. Drogo Castle is just up the road and all the varied delights of Dartmoor National Park are on your doorstep. *Directions:* From Exeter take the A38 to the A382, Bovey Tracy, turnoff. Turn left in Moretonhampstead onto the Princetown road, then immediately left (at the newsagents) to North Bovey. Go straight through the village down the hill and take the first right for the ¼-mile drive to Blackaller.

BLACKALLER
Owners: Hazel Phillips & Peter Hunt
North Bovey
Devon TQ13 8QY, England
Tel: (01647) 440322, Fax: (0131) 441131
Email: peter@blackaller.fsbusiness.co.uk
5 rooms
£38–£40 per person, dinner £24 (not Sun or Mon)
Open Mar to Dec, Credit cards: none
Children over 12
www.karenbrown.com/england/blackaller.html

Set in the picturesque moorland village of North Bovey, frequent winner of the best-kept Dartmoor village award, Gate House has a lovely location just behind the tree-lined village green. The location and warm welcome offered by hosts Sheila and John Williams add up to the perfect recipe for a countryside holiday. The sitting room has an ancient bread oven tucked inside a massive granite fireplace beneath a low, beamed ceiling, and the adjacent dining room has a large oak table in front of an atmospheric old stove. A narrow stairway leads up from the dining room to two of the guest bedrooms, each with a neat bathroom tucked under the eaves. The third bedroom is found at the top of another little staircase, this one off the sitting room, and affords views through a huge copper beech to the swimming pool (unheated), which guests are welcome to use, and idyllic green countryside. Sheila prepares a lovely country breakfast and a four-course evening meal (including vegetarian dishes if requested). Apart from walking on the moor and touring the moorland villages, guests enjoy visiting the many nearby National Trust properties. The Devon coastline is easily accessible and many guests take a day trip into Cornwall, often venturing as far afield as Clovelly. *Directions:* From Exeter take the A38 to the A382, Bovey Tracy, turnoff. Turn left in Mortenhampstead onto the Princetown road, then immediately left again to North Bovey. Go down the lane into the village and Gate House is on the left beyond the Ring of Bells.

GATE HOUSE
Owners: Sheila & John Williams
North Bovey
Devon TQ13 8RB, England
Tel & fax: (01647) 440479
Email: gatehouseondartmoor@talk21.com
3 rooms
£29–£31 per person, dinner £17
Open all year, Credit cards: none
Children over 15, No-smoking house
www.karenbrown.com/england/gatehouse.html

Tony Godel and Royd Laidlow have transformed this large, detached, Victorian merchant's house, just five minutes by bus or taxi from the center of Oxford, into a bed and breakfast gem. Burlington House is impeccably maintained and its rooms are immaculately decorated. Contemporary design featuring plain walls with touches of color and designer fabrics reigns throughout. The overall effect is luxurious and inviting but uncluttered and functional. Nine guestrooms in the house are supplemented by two across the Japanese-influenced, walled courtyard. Bathrooms are fabulously modern, with power showers, glass, and tile, and each one is artfully crafted in the space available. Breakfast is served in the cozy ground-floor dining room, dominated by its turn-of-the-century German Arts and Crafts dresser, its walls decorated with blue ironstone pottery and large framed prints of exotic fruits. The accent is on freshness, with real orange juice, vine-ripened tomatoes, homemade granola, and breads and cookies direct from the kitchen. Take the bus into Oxford and drop by the Tourist Information Centre at Gloucester Green for sightseeing suggestions (the town deserves several days of exploration). Be sure to visit nearby Woodstock and Blenheim Palace. *Directions:* Leave the M40 at Junction 8 for Oxford and follow the dual carriageway to the A40, northern by-pass. At the next roundabout take the first exit (to Summertown) into Banbury Road. Burlington House (number 374) is on the left after about half a mile.

BURLINGTON HOUSE   New
Owners: Tony Godel & Royd Laidlow
374 Banbury Road
Oxford OX2 7PP, England
Tel: (01865) 513513, Fax: (01865) 311785
Email: stay@burlington-house.co.uk
11 rooms
£37–£50 per person
Closed Christmas, Credit cards: all major
Children 12 & over, No-smoking house
www.karenbrown.com/england/burlingtonhouse.html

The sparkling condition of this modern suburban home just 2 miles from the historic heart of Oxford won me over completely. It is conveniently located near a bus stop, but you can also walk or bike into town. Alan, the resident manager, offers a warm welcome and is more than happy to supply guests with maps of the city and point them in the right direction for enjoying all the historic sites. Everything about the bedrooms here is of the highest standards: each is equipped with either a double, twin, or a double and twin beds, and shower room, and is kitted out with a small refrigerator, tea and coffee tray, biscuits, chocolates, and wine glasses—everything you need to make you feel at home. I was particularly impressed by the spacious ground-floor double room (room 7) and rooms 5 and 1, which contain both a double and a single bed. Cotswold House is included in an Inspector Morse detective book, *The Way Through the Woods*. A hearty breakfast (traditional English or vegetarian) is the only meal served. For dinner guests are directed to several local restaurants. Leave your car in the forecourt and take the bus into town. Alan suggests that your first port of call be the Tourist Information Centre, which is also the starting point for informative two-hour walking tours. *Directions:* Cotswold House is on the left, on the A4165, Banbury Road, 2 miles from the center of Oxford.

COTSWOLD HOUSE
Manager: Alan Clarke
363 Banbury Road
Oxford OX2 7PL, England
Tel & fax: (01865) 310558
Email: d.r.walker@talk21.com
7 rooms
£35–£37.50 per person
Open all year, Credit cards: MC, VS
Children over 6, No-smoking house
www.karenbrown.com/england/cotswoldhouse.html

Take a beautifully furnished 400-year-old farmhouse, add a 500-year-old threshing barn, an old cider shed complete with the press and horse-driven equipment, glorious gardens, acres of apple orchards, and caring hosts and you have ample reason to come to Cokesputt House in the rural Devonshire village of Payhembury. Enjoy a welcoming cup of tea in the drawing room or toast your toes in front of a log-burning fire in the comfortable parlor on a chilly evening. Bring your own wine to accompany dinner round the polished dining table beneath an ancient hewn beam that was once the centerpiece of the farmhouse kitchen, or let Caroline and Angus suggest an excellent pub in one of the nearby villages. Bedrooms are very attractive and you can choose from a spacious twin-bedded, double-bedded, or single room, each accompanied by an en-suite bath or shower room. Angus and Caroline are ardent gardeners who love discussing their own garden and directing guests to the vast number of notable gardens that lie within an hour's drive. Apple orchards on the property enable Angus to produce his own cider using the 100-year-old equipment he has restored in his cider shed. *Directions:* From the M5 exit 28 take the A373 towards Honiton and after 6 miles turn right to Payhembury. In the village turn sharp right opposite the Anglo garage, signposted Tale—Cokesputt House is on the right after 300 yards.

COKESPUTT HOUSE
Owners: Caroline & Angus Forbes
Payhembury
Honiton
Devon EX14 0HD, England
Tel: (0140) 4841289, Fax: (0870) 1642511
3 rooms
£34 per person, dinner £22.50
Closed Christmas & Jan
Credit cards: all major
Children over 12, No-smoking house

Hayes Farmhouse is no longer a working farm but the home of Julia and Thierry Sebline and their friendly golden retriever, Flora. The house was built in 1490 as a single-story hall house and expanded over the years to the substantial home you see today. Guests eat before the huge inglenook fireplace and relax in the spacious sitting room overlooking the garden. Julia is happy, with advance notice, to provide dinner and guests can bring their own wine to accompany the meal. A spacious double-bedded room has a small en-suite shower/bathroom and views across the valley to idyllic countryside, while the two other twin-bedded rooms have their private bathroom directly next door. Hayes Farmhouse provides a serene contrast to the bustle of nearby Rye. Just beyond Rye lies Winchelsea, one of the earliest examples of town planning, having been rebuilt in 1277 after being devastated by the marauding French. Inland lies Bodiam Castle, a small, picturesque castle surrounded by a wide moat, built by Richard II to secure the area against the French. Garden lovers head for Great Dixter and Sissinghurst. Farther afield lies Canterbury. *Directions:* From Rye take the B2089 towards Battle for 5 miles to Udimore where you turn right, signposted Peasmarsh and Beckley. After a mile turn right into Hayes Lane and Hayes Farmhouse is half a mile down Hayes Lane on the left up the driveway behind the Oast House.

HAYES FARMHOUSE
Owners: Julia & Thierry Sebline
Hayes Lane
Peasmarsh, Rye
East Sussex TN31 6XR, England
Tel: (01424) 882345, Fax: (01424) 882876
3 rooms
£35–£40 per person, dinner £18
Closed Christmas, Credit cards: none
Children over 6

Penryn is a very much a working town whose main thoroughfare, Broad Street, runs up the hill from the fishing quay. Halfway up the hill, fronting directly onto the street, you find Clare House. Built in the 17th century as an impressive gentleman's residence, it was restored several years ago by Jean and Jack Hewitt who ran the town's newsagents for many years. Jean is chatty and friendly and, while guests have their own spacious sitting room, she often whisks them to her side of the house where she and Jack join them for tea and a chat in their sitting room or in the Victorian conservatory with its hundred-year-old grapevine. Jean finds that having bed-and-breakfast guests has expanded her circle of friends from the town to the world. An enthusiastic artist, her watercolors are displayed around the house. Front bedrooms are particularly large: one has its shower cubicle and sink in the room and the loo across the hall while the other has its private bathroom across the hall. The third bedroom is quietly located at the back of the house and has en-suite facilities. A small refreshment room stocked with tea, coffee, soft drinks, and biscuits is located between the bedrooms. Guests often walk to the Waterfront restaurant or drive to the Pandora, an adorable thatched inn overlooking Restronguet Creek. *Directions:* From Truro, take the A39 towards Falmouth. Follow the second signpost to Penryn and turn right at the traffic lights on the quay into Broad Street—Clare House is on the left.

CLARE HOUSE
Owners: Jean & Jack Hewitt
20 Broad Street
Penryn
Cornwall TR10 8JH, England
Tel: (01326) 373294, Fax: none
3 rooms
£25–£27 per person
Closed Christmas & New Year, Credit cards: none
Children over 12, No-smoking house
www.karenbrown.com/england/clarehouse.html

Christine and Charles Taylor feel very lucky to live in some of most beautiful countryside in Cornwall, looking down across fields to the sea and St. Michael's Mount. Their farmhouse is a barn painstakingly renovated over several years. Inside, beamed ceilings, whitewashed granite walls, and flagstone floors all contribute to the traditional farmhouse look. The Pink Room in the main house has its four-poster bed decked out in crisp white linen and its adjoining bathroom has a central bath. Just across the courtyard are two more lovely rooms—Apricot, all dainty and delicious and, my personal favorite, the most spacious Blue Room with its large bathroom and French windows opening onto a private terrace with views across the fields to Perranuthnoe and the sea. Breakfast is served at the 9-foot-long oak refectory table in the open-plan family room/kitchen, which occupies the entire upstairs of the barn. For dinner it is just a short walk across the fields to Perranuthnoe and the Victoria Inn. There are dozens of interesting places to visit in the area, from photogenic fishing villages to sub-tropical gardens. You must not miss the island of St. Michael's Mount, reached by a causeway at low tide, otherwise in small boats. St. Ives, a former fishing village, is home to a branch of the Tate Gallery. *Directions:* From the A30 after the Crowlas roundabout take the A394 towards Helston. A quarter mile after the next roundabout take the first right towards Perranuthnoe and the first left, which leads to Ednovean Farm.

EDNOVEAN FARM
Owners: Christine & Charles Taylor
Perranuthnoe, Penzance
Cornwall TR20 9LZ, England
Tel: (01736) 711883, Fax: (01736) 710480
Email: info@ednoveanfarm.co.uk
3 rooms
£27.50–£35 per person
Closed Christmas, Credit cards: none
Children over 16
www.karenbrown.com/england/ednovean.html

No railroad noise for the lord of the manor in this neighborhood—he lobbied for the Petworth train station to be built beyond earshot, almost 2 miles from town. The last train ran in 1966 and the gingerbread-style Victorian station was cleverly converted to a home several years later. The former waiting room is now the most spacious of sitting rooms, with sofas gathered round the fire and individual pine tables set for breakfast on cool days. Warmer days find guests breakfasting outside on the platform beside the sweep of lawn that was once the train tracks. Two bedrooms occupy one side of the building—downstairs a brass-and-iron queen-sized bed and spacious modern shower room and upstairs an equally romantic room set beneath a soaring beamed ceiling with high skylights instead of windows. A further four are found in two Edwardian Pullman cars (as used on the Orient Express) sitting in the siding. They have been restored to reflect an era of unrestrained luxury. Breakfast is the only meal served so guests often pop next door to The Badger pub for dinner. Petworth is an ideal base for exploring stately homes (Petworth, Goodwood, Uppark), viewing gorgeous gardens (Westdean, Nymans), and visiting the Weald and Downland Museum. *Directions:* From Guildford take the A3, Portsmouth road, to Milford, the A283 to Petworth, and leave Petworth on the A285, Chichester road. After 1½ miles The Badger pub is on your left. Take the slip road in front of the pub—this leads to The Old Railway Station.

THE OLD RAILWAY STATION
Owners: Lou & Mike Rapley
Petworth
West Sussex GU28 0JF, England
Tel & fax: (01798) 342346
Email: mlr@old-station.co.uk
6 rooms
£42.50–£49 per person
Open all year, Credit cards: MC, VS
Children over 16, No-smoking house
www.karenbrown.com/england/oldrailway.html

There was a farm on this site recorded in the Domesday Book of 1086, though the present farm and its outbuildings date from the 1500s. Anthony's family have farmed here for generations and, while he concentrates on all things farming, Lynne concentrates on the upscale bed and breakfast that she runs in a wing of the farmhouse and the converted barns. Her accommodation is not your typical farmhouse style: the rooms I saw were furnished with pastel-painted furniture coordinating with the draperies and bedspreads, giving a light, airy feel. Bathrooms and shower rooms are sparklingly modern and one sports a claw-foot tub and separate shower. Lynne loves to eat out and enjoys discussing dining plans with guests. She also has a folder on restaurants and traditional pubs in the area. Lynne directed us to Tencreek Farm for a scrumptious Cornish cream tea in the prettiest of gardens. If you are planning on staying for a week, consider renting the adorable little cottage for two overlooking the cow pasture. Decorated in vibrant Mediterranean colors, the cottage is excellently equipped for a romantic getaway. The idyllically pretty seaside villages of Fowey, Looe, and Polperro are great attractions as are the National Trust houses of Cotehele and Lanhydrock. The spectacular Eden Project is approximately 30 minutes away by car. *Directions:* From Looe take the A387 signposted Polperro. Before you reach Polperro, Trenderway Farm is signposted to your right.

TRENDERWAY FARM
Owners: Lynne & Anthony Tuckett
Pelynt
Polperro
Cornwall PL13 2LY, England
Tel: (01503) 272214, Fax: (01503) 272991
Email: trenderwayfarm@hotmail.com
4 rooms
£30–£35 per person
Closed Christmas, Credit cards: MC, VS
Children over 16, No-smoking house
www.karenbrown.com/england/trenderway.html

A humorous, tongue-in-cheek "rule" book is found in every bedroom at Bales Mead and woe betide you if you do not comply! The illustrations are drawn by Peter Clover who, with his partner Stephen Blue, runs a very tight ship in their exceptionally attractive home. Guests enjoy a sophisticated sitting room complete with log-burning fireplace and baby grand piano. Upstairs, the bedrooms are named after villages in the Porlock Vale. Selworthy is cool in lemon and blue with outstanding ocean views. Bossington is all in café au lait, white, and mulberry with a view of the shingle beach and distant headland. Both Selworthy and Bossington have their own private bathrooms. Allerford (a smaller room overlooking the garden and woodlands) is used in conjunction with one of the other rooms by larger parties who do not mind sharing a bathroom. Breakfast is the only meal served (promptly at 9 am)—Stephen and Peter recommend excellent local pubs and restaurants for dinner. In the '50s the house was owned by a well-known horticulturist who filled the garden with specimen plants from all over the world. Just across the lane are vast stretches of shingle beach. Bales Mead is in the hamlet of West Porlock between the pretty village of Porlock and the picturesque harbor of Porlock Weir. Rising behind the house are the vast expanses of Exmoor. *Directions:* From Minehead take the A39 to Porlock, then a right turn to Porlock Weir takes you a short distance to West Porlock, where you find Bales Mead on the left.

BALES MEAD
Owners: Stephen Blue & Peter Clover
West Porlock
Somerset TA24 8NX, England
Tel: (01643) 862565, Fax: (01643) 862544
3 rooms
£37.50 per person
Closed Christmas & New Year, Credit cards: none
Children over 14, No-smoking house

The lifeboatman has been known to deliver guests to Fortitude Cottage when there's an especially high tide. While this is an adventure for visitors, Maggie and Mike take the sea coming up the road as a natural part of living beside the harbor in Old Portsmouth. When she suspects the sea may be paying a visit, Maggie simply removes the rugs from the tile floor in the little downstairs bedroom and mops the floor when the tide ebbs. This attractive room is decorated in pink candy stripes and has a small en-suite shower room. Curl up on the window seat in the airy upstairs sitting room and watch the Isle of Wight ferries and the fishing boats come and go. On the top floor two small pretty bedrooms have tiny en-suite shower rooms (the front room has a harbor view). For dinner, Maggie makes suggestions on the pubs and restaurants within walking distance. Take the waterbus (Easter to November) across the harbor to tour Nelson's flagship, *HMS Victory*, Henry VIII's ship, *Mary Rose*, and *HMS Warrior,* an 1861 iron-clad battleship, then go on to the submarine museum. *Directions:* Exit the M27 at junction 12, signposted Portsmouth and ferries. Follow signs for the Isle of Wight car ferry through the center of the town, then look for a brown signpost (at a roundabout) to the cathedral and Old Portsmouth. Pass the cathedral and at the end of the road turn right. Fortitude Cottage is on your left.

FORTITUDE COTTAGE
Owners: Maggie & Mike Hall
51 Broad Street
Old Portsmouth
Hampshire PO1 2JD, England
Tel & fax: (02392) 823748
Email: fortcott@aol.com
3 rooms
£25 per person
Closed Christmas, Credit cards: MC, VS
Children over 12, No-smoking house
www.karenbrown.com/england/fortitudecottage.html

The Burgoyne family were people of substance hereabouts for they secured the premier building site in this picturesque Swaledale village and built an impressive home that dwarfs the surrounding buildings. Gone are the days when one family could justify such a large home and now it's a welcoming hotel run by Derek Hickson and Peter Carwardine. Derek makes guests feel thoroughly at home while Peter makes certain that they live up to their motto, "Tis substantial happiness to eat." Peter prepares a fixed-price, four-course meal every evening with plenty of choices for each course. The handsome lounge is warmed by a log fire in winter and full of inviting books on the area. There's abundant scope for walking and driving in this rugged area using Reeth as your base, though you'll be hard pressed to find a lovelier dales view than the one from your bedroom window of stone-walled fields rising to vast moorlands (one bedroom faces the back of the house). Redmire, being more spacious, is the premier room, while Marrick is a most luxurious four-poster suite. Robes and slippers are provided for the occupants of Keld, Grinton, and Thwaite who have to slip across the hall to their bathrooms. Richmond with its medieval castle and the Bowes Museum, near Barnard Castle, with its fine collection of French furniture and porcelain, are added attractions. *Directions:* From Richmond take the A6108 towards Leyburn for 5 miles to the B6270 for the 5-mile drive to Reeth. The Burgoyne Hotel is on the village green.

THE BURGOYNE HOTEL
Owners: Derek Hickson & Peter Carwardine
Reeth
Yorkshire DL11 6SN, England
Tel & fax: (01748) 884292
Email: enquiries@theburgoyne.co.uk
8 rooms
£45–£75 per person, dinner £24.50
Open Feb 14 to Jan 2, Credit cards: MC, VS
Children over10
www.karenbrown.com/england/burgoyne.html

An unassuming street frontage gives nothing away of the treat that lies in store beyond the front door, for Millgate House is one of Richmond's finest Georgian homes. Faux-painted marble columns draw you through the wide hall into the drawing room packed with serendipitous heirlooms, finds, and antiques collected by Tim Culkin and Austin Lynch. Tall windows overlook the lush, secluded, award-winning garden that terraces down to the river far below. The same splendid view is enjoyed by the delightful dining room with its enviable antiques and monster pot plants. A bountiful offering of fruits heads up the breakfast menu. For dinner stroll across the square to the French Gate Café. The two premier bedrooms, a twin and a queen, face the river. Both are very large and beautifully furnished, and have spacious bathrooms and wonderful views. The third bedroom is at the front of the house and has a bathroom across the hall. A five-bedroom coach house beside the river and a two-bedroom apartment are available on a weekly basis. You are just steps from Richmond's cobbled market square and just down the road from the 11th-century Norman castle. Tours of the Yorkshire Dales and Moors and York itself give you an excuse to spend several nights here to soak up the atmosphere of this remarkable house and garden. *Directions: Directions:* From the A1, take the A6136 to Richmond. Head for the central Market Place where you find Millgate House at the bottom of the hill opposite Barclays Bank. Park in front to unload.

MILLGATE HOUSE
Owners: Tim Culkin & Austin Lynch
Richmond
North Yorkshire DL10 4JN, England
Tel: (01748) 823571, Fax: (01748) 850701
Email: oztim@millgatehouse.demon.co.uk
3 rooms, 1 cottage, 1 apartment
£35 per person, Cottage £554–£1,257 weekly
Apartment £241–£381 weekly
Open all year, Credit cards: none
Children over 10, No-smoking house
www.karenbrown.com/england/millgate.html

Whashton Springs Farm is a perfect base for exploring the Yorkshire Dales. A five-minute drive finds you at the foot of Swaledale in Richmond, with its cobbled market square and Norman castle perched high above the river. The farm is run by Gordon Turnbull and his two sons who grow corn and potatoes and run a herd of hill cows and sheep. Spring is an especially good time to visit, for the little lambs are kept close to the farm. Fairlie welcomes guests to the farmhouse and offers accommodation within the large, sturdy house or in one of the delightfully private bedrooms that open directly onto the courtyard. A wing of the barn has been converted into a most attractive self-catering cottage for families who want to stay for a week. Gordon serves a Yorkshire farmhouse breakfast, giving you an opportunity to ask questions about the farm, and directs guests to local pubs and restaurants in Richmond for dinner. Within an hour you can be in Durham, York, or the Lake District. The Yorkshire Dales are on your doorstep and the North Yorkshire Moors just half an hour distant. *Directions:* From the A1, take the A6136 to Richmond. Turn right at the traffic lights signposted for Ravensworth and follow this road for 3 miles to the farm, which is on your left at the bottom of a steep hill.

WHASHTON SPRINGS FARM
Owners: Fairlie & Gordon Turnbull
Richmond
North Yorkshire DL11 7JS
England
Tel: (01748) 822884, Fax: (01748) 826285
Email: washton@turnbullg-f.freeserve.co.uk
8 rooms, 1 cottage
£24–£26 per person
Open Feb to mid-Dec, Credit cards: none
Children over 5
www.karenbrown.com/england/whashtonspringsfarm.html

Few English guesthouses offer the ambiance, warmth, and welcome of Mizzards Farm, a lovely 16th-century farmhouse built of stone and brick. The setting is peaceful: the River Rother flows through the 13 acres of gardens and fields and the driveway winds through the large meadowlike front lawn past a small lake. The heart of the house, where breakfast is served, is especially inviting, with one wall filled by a massive inglenook fireplace and a staircase leading up to an open minstrels' gallery. In a newer wing, a sophisticated lounge is nicely furnished with antiques and highlighted by a grand piano. Concerts are held here twice a year. The home was previously owned by an English rock star who converted the largest bedroom into a glitzy, but fun, theatrical showplace with electric curtains operated from the bed on a grand dais and a marble bathroom featuring a double bathtub. The other two guestrooms are smaller and are pleasantly decorated in more traditional decor. Dinner is not served but there are many excellent choices of places to eat nearby. For the athletically minded, Mizzards also has a covered swimming pool for guests' use. *Directions:* From Petersfield take the A272 towards Midhurst. Turn right at the crossroads in Rogate, follow the road for half a mile, cross the narrow bridge over the river, and take the first right on the small lane up to Mizzards Farm.

MIZZARDS FARM
Owners: Harriet & Julian Francis
Rogate
Petersfield
Hampshire GU31 5HS, England
Tel: (01730) 821656, Fax: (01730) 821655
3 rooms
£30–£35 per person
Closed Christmas, Credit cards: none
Children over 8, No-smoking house

Rosedale Abbey nestles in a sheltered green valley below the gently rolling moorland. High above the village lies Thorgill, a few houses strung out along a narrow road just beneath the moor. Here you find Sevenford House, a sturdy home built at the turn of the century for the vicar of the village church, and now a private home. Linda found it the perfect place to raise her three elder sons and when they were grown, decided with her partner Ian to open their home to guests. The three large bedrooms are delightfully furnished and each has a snug en-suite shower room. Enjoy a welcoming cup of tea and a chat in the lovely drawing room and browse through the books that highlight the many things to do in this lovely part of Yorkshire. Ride a steam train on the North Yorkshire Moors Railway, visit the vast array of stately homes, explore the lovely villages nestled beneath the moor, and visit the coastside towns of Whitby, Runswick Bay, and Robin Hood's Bay. It's walking country and just above the house you can follow the path of an old railway line that takes you on a spectacular four-hour walk along the moor with views of Rosedale valley. *Directions:* From Pickering take the A170 towards Helmsley for 3 miles, then turn right for the 7-mile drive to Rosedale. Just as you enter the village, turn sharp left and go up the hill to the White Horse Hotel where you turn right (signposted Thorgill). Sevenford House is the first house on your right.

SEVENFORD HOUSE
Owners: Linda Sugars & Ian Thompson
Thorgill, Rosedale Abbey, near Pickering
North Yorkshire YO18 8SE, England
Tel: (01751) 417283, Fax: (01751) 417505
Email: sevenford@aol.com
3 rooms
£22.50 per person
Closed Christmas, Credit cards: none
Children welcome, No-smoking house
www.karenbrown.com/england/sevenford.html

With a backdrop of mountain peaks and a lush green lawn sweeping down towards Rosthwaite village, this award-winning establishment has a superb location in Borrowdale, one of the loveliest and quietest Lake District valleys. Reputedly the house was built in 1850 as a dream home for an American returning to England after making his fortune. Brenda and Glen Davies have recently renovated this large Victorian residence, adding sparkling deluxe bath and shower rooms to all of the bedrooms and decorating the entire house in a delightful way that is totally in keeping with its period charm and character. All the rooms are comfortable, light, airy, and uncluttered. The bedrooms are named after nearby mountains and vary from spacious to snug, though even the snuggest has a corner to accommodate comfortable chairs and a TV. After a day out walking or sightseeing, relax over a drink in the sitting room before one of Brenda's excellent dinners where homemade soups, sauces, and decadent desserts are her specialty. This is walking country so the hotel has a drying and ironing room for clothing. Just behind the house, overlooking the garden, is a delightful little self-catering cottage for two people. An excellent day out is to drive high over the adjacent pass to Buttermere and Crummock Water. Visit Wordsworth House in Cockermouth, drive along Bassenthwaite Lake to Keswick, and after sightseeing, continue along Derwent Water back to Rosthwaite. *Directions:* Hazel Bank is 7 miles south of Keswick on the B5289. Turn left over the little humpbacked bridge just before entering Rosthwaite village.

HAZEL BANK
Owners: Brenda & Glen Davies
Rosthwaite, Borrowdale, Keswick
Cumbria CA12 5XB, England
Tel: (017687) 77248, Fax: (017687) 77373
Email: enquiries@hazelbankhotel.co.uk
8 rooms
£46.50–£64.50 per person dinner, B&B
Open all year, Credit cards: MC, VS
Children over 10, No-smoking house
www.karenbrown.com/england/hazelbank.html

The Roseland Peninsula is one of Cornwall's loveliest areas, a maze of meandering narrow lanes, quaint villages, and exquisite coastal scenery. Set almost in the center of the peninsula you find one of Cornwall's loveliest homes, Crugsillick, a Queen Anne manor house extended in 1710 from an Elizabethan farmhouse, the beautiful home of Rosemary and Oliver Barstow. Guests help themselves to very reasonably priced drinks in the gracious drawing room whose lovely plasterwork ceiling was created by captive French prisoners of the Napoleonic wars. The Barstows often join their guests for dinner. The blue bedroom is very spacious and its king-sized bed can be made into twins. The pink room has a queen-sized bed and its bathroom across the hall, while the yellow room has twin beds and a small shower room. Guests often walk to the beach via a narrow smugglers' lane and enjoy walks along the coast. Gardens abound, the most popular being the Lost Gardens of Heligan, a recently restored garden that had been abandoned for many years and the Eden Project, the largest greenhouse in the world. *Directions:* From St. Austell take the B3287 signposted St. Mawes to Tregony where you turn left on the B3275 through Ruan High Lanes. After ¼ mile turn left for Veryan and enter Crugsillick through the third white gate on your right over a cattle grid.

CRUGSILLICK MANOR
Owners: Rosemary & Oliver Barstow
Ruan High Lanes
Cornwall TR2 5LJ, England
Tel: (01872) 501214, Fax: (01872) 501228
Email: rmb@adtelfree.com
3 rooms, 3 cottages
£40–£48 per person, dinner £25
Closed Christmas & New Year, Credit cards: MC, VS
Children over 12
www.karenbrown.com/england/crugsillickmanor.html

We found Lizzie Newton weeding a flowerbed in her prize-winning garden, which looks out over peaceful fields. The same combination of care and flair that Lizzie displays in her garden she applies to her delightful thatched cottage where she welcomes guests. The comfortable twin-bedded guest bedroom is bright and cheery and accompanied by an en-suite shower room. In the evening guests are welcome to join Lizzie in her comfortable sitting room. The "rogues' gallery" of old and recent family photos on the staircase is often a talking point for Lizzie and her guests. Breakfast is the only meal served in the dining room and while you can walk across the fields to the Charlton Cat, there are lots of delightful pubs within easy driving distance. Just up the road is the picturesque village of Pewsey. Less than a half-hour drive finds you wandering amongst the ancient stones of Avebury and Stonehenge, wondering why Bronze Age man spent what has been estimated at millions of manhours constructing such temples. Another local phenomenon is crop circles, mysterious, elaborate patterns that appear overnight in crop fields. Much more down-to-earth are Georgian Bath, Salisbury with its exquisite cathedral, and the handsome town of Marlborough with its Georgian buildings and little alleys of old timbered cottages. *Directions:* From Marlborough take the A345 towards Amesbury to Pewsey (8 miles) and 2 miles after Pewsey, turn for Devizes at a small roundabout with the Woodbridge Arms on your right. On reaching Rushall go past the school and Little Thatch is on your left.

LITTLE THATCH
Owner: Elizabeth Newton
Rushall, Pewsey
Wiltshire SN9 6EN, England
Tel & fax: (01980) 635282
1 room
£22.50 per person
Open Apr to Jan, Credit cards: none
Children welcome, No-smoking house
www.karenbrown.com/england/littlethatch.html

Rye, a busy port in medieval times, has become marooned 2 miles inland since the sea receded. Once the haunt of smugglers who climbed the narrow cobbled streets laden with booty from France, Rye is now a picturesque town that invites tourists to walk its cobbled lanes. On Rye's most historic street, Jeake's House dates back to 1690 when it was built by Samuel Jeake as a wool storehouse (wool was smuggled to France while brandy, lace, and salt were brought into England). From the street you enter a small reception area, which leads to a Victorian parlor and bar. This opens up to a large galleried hall, now the dining room, where a roaring log fire blazes in winter. At some point in its history the house was owned by the Baptist Church who built this room as a chapel. From the spacious attic bedroom to the romantic four-poster room and the snug single, no two rooms are alike. All are most attractively decorated and furnished with antiques in keeping with the historical mood of the house. All offer modern amenities such as tea-making trays, television, and telephone and all but two have en-suite bathrooms. Within easy driving distance are Winchelsea, Battle Abbey (built on the site of the Battle of Hastings in 1066), Bodiam Castle, and Sissinghurst Gardens. *Directions:* Rye is between Folkestone and Hastings on the A259. Mermaid Street is the town's main street—park in front to unload and you will be directed to nearby private parking.

JEAKE'S HOUSE
Owner: Jenny Hadfield
Mermaid Street, Rye
East Sussex TN31 7ET, England
Tel: (01797) 222828, Fax: (01797) 222623
Email: jeakeshouse@btinternet.com
12 rooms
£31.50–£51.50 per person
Open all year, Credit cards: MC, VS
Children over 12
www.karenbrown.com/england/jeakeshouse.html

Rye is one of England's most enchanting towns and Little Orchard House is one of Rye's most engaging small bed and breakfasts. The location is ideal, right in the heart of town on a small lane leading off Mermaid Street. Don't miss the inn's discreet sign. An archway frames a most inviting little courtyard faced by a pretty cottage with a red-colored door. Inside there is no formal reception area: registration takes place in the cozy, country-style kitchen, which opens onto a very large old-fashioned walled garden. In one corner rises a red-brick tower, once used by smugglers to signal if the coast was clear. The bedrooms, both four-posters, are most attractive: the Garden Room is romantic and the Hayloft cottagey with pine and wicker. The very friendly owners, Sara and Robert, are very involved in the management of their bed and breakfast and personally see that each guest is made welcome and pampered. To learn more about Rye's fascinating history, attend the sound and light show at the Rye Town Model, then set out to explore with a walking tour of the town. *Directions:* Follow signs to the town center and enter via the old Landgate Arch. West Street is the third street on the left off the High Street (ignore the "Authorized traffic only" signs). Park in front to unload and you will be directed to nearby private parking.

LITTLE ORCHARD HOUSE
Owners: Sara Brinkhurst & Robert Bird
West Street
Rye
East Sussex TN31 7ES, England
Tel & fax: (01797) 223831
Email: sara.brinkhurst@virgin.net
2 rooms
£32–£45 per person
Open all year, Credit cards: MC, VS
Children over 12
www.karenbrown.com/england/littleorchardhouse.html

Atop the quaint cobbled streets of Rye you find the ancient church and churchyard of St. Mary's, surrounded by a square of delightful old houses. Fortunately for visitors to this picturesque town, one of these, The Old Vicarage (a dusty-pink Georgian house with white trim and twin chimneys), is run as a guesthouse by a delightful young couple, Julia and Paul Masters. You can be certain of a proper cuppa here as Julia is a tea-blender and has devised a special blend of tea for her guests. Since Julia and Paul bought The Old Vicarage, they have been constantly upgrading and refurbishing the guestrooms, all of which are decorated with Laura Ashley fabrics. Two bedrooms have contemporary four-poster beds, one has a coronet-style draped headboard, and tucked under the eaves on the top floor is a two-bedroom suite. The garden suite, a large family room with a sitting area, is below stairs. Each of the rooms has color television, hairdryer, and hospitality tray that includes homemade fudge and biscuits—not good for the figure but much appreciated with a cup of tea after sightseeing. The ambiance throughout this bed and breakfast is one of homey comfort. Overnight parking is available in a small private car park nearby. If you write ahead, the Masters will send you a brochure with a map on just how to find them amongst the maze of Rye's streets. Rye deserves a visit of several days to explore its narrow, cobbled streets, shops, and old fortifications. *Directions:* Rye is on the A259 between Folkestone and Hastings.

THE OLD VICARAGE GUEST HOUSE
Owners: Julia & Paul Masters
66 Church Square, Rye
East Sussex TN31 7HF, England
Tel: (01797) 222119, Fax: (01797) 227466
5 rooms
£35–£52 per person
Closed Christmas, Credit cards: none
Children over 8

Jane and Steven Epperson lived in both America and England (he's a Texan, she's English) before deciding to settle in Cornwall, where they bought Anchorage House as the shell of an impressive home and finished it off in a grand Georgian style. Furnished throughout in antiques, the home has the advantage of having a traditional feel accompanied by all the luxurious modern conveniences of king- or queen-sized beds, satellite television, individually controlled central heating, power showers, and generous-sized baths. Guests often relax in the conservatory where breakfast is taken overlooking the garden, lap pool, and Jacuzzi. Jane is happy to offer the occasional dinner round the antique dining-room table or direct guests to the excellent pubs and restaurants within a few minutes' walk or drive. Anchorage House's location on a quiet cul-de-sac just off the A390 makes it ideal for those who want to avoid navigating narrow Cornish lanes to reach their accommodation and also means that it is handily placed for making driving forays to places as near as the Eden Project (just outside the village) or the Lost Gardens of Heligan (15 minutes' drive), and as far away as Land's End and St. Michael's Mount (1 hour's drive). *Directions:* Anchorage House is just off the A390, 1 mile west of St. Blazey, 2 miles east of St. Austell. Opposite the St. Austell Garden Center turn into a small lane signposted Tregrehan and then immediately left into a driveway leading to Anchorage House.

ANCHORAGE HOUSE
Owners: Jane & Steven Epperson
Nettles Corner, Tregrehan, St. Austell
Cornwall PL25 3RH, England
Tel: (01726) 814071, Fax: none
Email: stay@anchoragehouse.co.uk
3 rooms
£32–£39 per person, dinner £25
Open all year, Credit cards: MC, VS
Children over 16, No-smoking house
www.karenbrown.com/england/anchorage.html

This lovely Georgian home set in 5 acres of grounds in peaceful countryside offers outstanding accommodations. Rashleigh is an enormous room, its double bed having an artfully draped bedhead matching the curtains and bedspread; Treffry has a 6-foot bed that can be two single beds; and Prideaux has a dainty white four-poster. Each bedroom has an elegant en-suite bathroom with spa bath, tea- and coffee-makings, television, telephone, and a huge umbrella for guests to use during their stay. Guests have their own entrance into a lofty hallway where double doors open up to a vast sitting room all decked out in warm shades of pale green. Beyond lies a sunny conservatory with wicker chairs and little tables set for breakfast, the only meal served. Candid reviews of local restaurants enable guests to decide where they would like to eat, with choices ranging from formal restaurants to a pub on the beach in a smugglers' cove. Outside are vast lawns, a swimming pool, a hot tub, and a paved terrace with spectacular views across rolling countryside. Local attractions include the picturesque town of Fowey, the fishing village of Mevagissey, and National Trust properties such as Lanhydrock. The Eden Project is only 3 miles away. *Directions:* Pass over the Tamar Bridge into Cornwall and follow signs to Liskeard. Take the A390 (St. Austell turnoff), following it through Lostwithiel and into St. Blazey. Cross the railway lines and opposite the Jet garage turn right into Prideaux Road, following it up the hill to Nanscawen on your right.

NANSCAWEN MANOR HOUSE
Owners: Fiona & Keith Martin
Prideaux Road, Luxulyan Valley, St. Blazey
Cornwall PL24 2SR, England
Tel & fax: (01726) 814488
Email: keith@nanscawen.com
3 rooms
£30–£44 per person
Open: all year, Credit cards: MC, VS
Children over 12, No-smoking house
www.karenbrown.com/england/nanscawenhouse.html

Breathtaking, panoramic views of the Wye Valley open up from Cinderhill House, a pink-washed house whose core dates back to the 14th century with additions over the years. Gillie is a warm and friendly hostess who enjoys welcoming guests to her home. Bedrooms in the main house are very prettily decorated and all have tea and coffee trays. At the end of the drive Cider Cottage, the converted coach house, is available on either a bed-and-breakfast or self-catering basis. Breakfast is a treat: fruit compotes and cold cereals are followed by hot dishes such as fresh salmon fishcakes and herb omelets, yet Gillie considers dinner her forte! On chilly evenings a crackling log fire invites guests into the large sitting room to enjoy a drink before dinner. Apart from enjoying the peace and quiet of the Wye Valley and the Forest of Dean, guests venture farther afield to Bristol, Cardiff, Gloucester, Cheltenham, Bath, and Hereford. *Directions:* Take the M4 from Bristol towards Chepstow over the old Severn Bridge using the M48 and take exit 22 for Monmouth. Take the A466 for 10 miles, then turn right over the Bigsweir Bridge for St. Briavels. Follow the road up and the house is on the left just before the castle.

CINDERHILL HOUSE
Owner: Gillie Peacock
St. Briavels
Gloucestershire GL15 6RH, England
Tel: (01594) 530393, Fax: (01594) 530098
Email: cinderhill.house@virgin.net
4 rooms, 1 cottage
£31–£45 per person, dinner from £16
Closed Christmas, Credit cards: none
Children welcome
www.karenbrown.com/england/cinderhill.html

Surrounded by open farmland on the edge of the Vale of Evesham, Salford Farm House dates back to the 19th century and showcases many of the original architectural features such as beams, flagstones, and fireplaces. It is traditionally decorated with antiques and family heirlooms and silverware gleams on the dining-room table. A contented herd of ceramic cow creamers sits on the windowsill. A fascinating collection of French costume prints bedecks the hall stairs leading to two double (or twin) bedrooms, both with modern bathrooms en suite, one pink, one cream, the latter with its own separate dressing room. On arrival guests are invited to afternoon tea in the sitting room before a roaring fire or, on warmer, sun-dappled days, in the flower-filled garden. Jane prepares sumptuous breakfasts and dinners on her Aga in the country kitchen. Fresh local produce—fruits, vegetables, meat, and game from the Marquess of Hertford's Ragley Estate—features largely on the menu. Salford Farm House is just 8 miles from Stratford-upon-Avon and 15 miles from Warwick Castle. Ragley Hall, Kenilworth, the Cotswolds, and an abundance of National Trust properties are nearby. *Directions*: From Stratford-upon-Avon or Evesham take the A46, following signs to Salford Priors. Turn right opposite the church in the center of the village (signposted Dunnington). Salford Farm House is approximately 1 mile along on the right.

SALFORD FARM HOUSE   New
Owners: Jane Gibson & Richard Beach
Salford Priors
Worcestershire WR11 5SG, England
Tel: (01386) 870000, Fax: (01386) 870300
Email: salfordfarmhouse@aol.com
2 rooms
£35 per person, dinner £25
Closed Christmas & New Year, Credit cards: MC, VS
Children 12 & over, No-smoking house
www.karenbrown.com/england/salfordfarmhouse.html

Tim knows how to look after guests: for many years he was the manager (and one of the owners) of Number Sixteen, one of London's splendid little townhouse hotels. After selling his share of the hotel, he came back to his native Devon to run Parford Well. Set within a walled garden, the comfortable house is totally dedicated to guest accommodation while Tim lives in the tiny adjoining cottage. Sink into the oh-so-comfortable sofa in the sitting room and toast your toes before the fire. The decor is of such a high standard that, apart from the smaller proportions of the house, you would think you are in a grand country house hotel. Breakfast is the only meal served round the farmhouse table in the dining room. If you want complete seclusion, ask to eat in the tiny private dining room with grand draperies that once belonged to the Queen Mother and just enough room for a table for two. Upstairs are three delightful small bedrooms, two en suite and one with its private bathroom across the hall. Tim is an expert on where to walk, what to see, and which tea shops and restaurants to frequent. He can suggest enough activities to keep you busy for a fortnight. *Directions:* From Moretonhampstead take the A382 towards Okehampton for 3 miles. Turn right at the Sandy Park crossroads towards Castle Drogo and Parford Well is 100 yards along on your left.

PARFORD WELL
Owner: Tim Daniel
Sandy Park
Chagford
Devon TQ13 8JW, England
Tel: (01647) 433353, Fax: none
3 rooms
£25–£33 per person
Open Mar to Dec 23, Credit cards: none
Children over 8, No-smoking house
www.karenbrown.com/england/parfordwell.html

Buffalo Bill came here for tea and was entertained like visiting royalty in the grand drawing room. While you may not be on a mission to buy Cleveland Bay horses, you too can enjoy this grand room, but I'd rather be relishing the country charm of all the other rooms in this 17th-century farmhouse. You see, the drawing room was built not to be enjoyed but as a room to impress those who came to buy horses. The horses are gone, replaced by cars—Jim Evans races cars and while he was attracted to the house's spacious accommodation for his vehicles, Joyce was attracted to its loveliness. There is plenty of room for guests to have their own wing, including the drawing room, so curl up with a book in the winter parlor and enjoy breakfast round the oak gate-leg table set before the fire. Breakfast usually includes lots of fruit from the garden. While Joyce cooks the occasional dinner in winter, guests usually pop down to the local pub, the Ham and Cheese, for an evening meal. The delightful bedrooms include a queen and a twin with snug en-suite showers and another queen-bedded room with a lovely bathroom just across the hall. York is a must and only a half-hour drive away. Closer at hand is Castle Howard, the vast, rather impersonal home of the Howard family. Much more cozy in size are Sledmere, Duncombe Park, and Nunnington, where Clive of India lived. *Directions:* From York take the A64 towards Scarborough. Pass Malton and after 3 miles turn right into Scagglethorpe—the Manor is on the left.

SCAGGLETHORPE MANOR
Owners: Joyce & Jim Evans
Main Street
Scagglethorpe, Malton
North Yorkshire YO17 8DT, England
Tel & fax: (01944) 758909
3 rooms
£24–£26 per person, dinner £18 (Oct to Apr)
Open all year, Credit cards: none
Children over 12

A cozy hilltop refuge from winter storms, an outstanding spring, summer, or autumn base for exploring Derbyshire by car or on foot, Dannah Farm is a delightful place for all seasons. The solid Georgian farmhouse is turned over entirely to guests, with delightful cottagey bedrooms and two cozy, tastefully furnished sitting rooms. I particularly liked the three suites, two of which have their private entries from the old stableyard. One has a snug sitting room with an open-tread spiral staircase leading to the low-beamed bedroom while the other is a lofty raftered room with a four-poster bed. Another part of the old stables is a convivial bar and country-style restaurant where guests enjoy breakfast and dinner and outside guests are welcomed on Saturday evenings. Adults and children love the animals—the squeaking baby kune kune pigs are a great attraction. The Peak District National Park is on your doorstep full of walks, bike trails, and appealing little villages. The stately homes of Haddon Hall and Chatsworth House are well worth a visit. *Directions:* From Belper take the A517 (Ashbourne road) for 2 miles and after the Hanging Gate Inn take the next right (at the top of the hill) to Shottle (1½ miles). Go straight at the crossroads and after 200 yards turn right into Dannah Farm.

DANNAH FARM
Owners: Joan & Martin Slack
Bowmans Lane
Shottle
Belper
Derbyshire DE56 2DR, England
Tel: (01773) 550273, Fax: (01773) 550590
Email: reservations@dannah.demon.co.uk
9 rooms
£39.50–£60 per person, dinner £19.50 (not Sun)
Closed Christmas, Credit cards: MC, VS
Children welcome
www.karenbrown.com/england/dannahfarm.html

Standing apart from the lovely village of Sinnington just beyond its ancient church, Hunters Hill, with its magnificent countryside views, was until recent times the home of the estate manager for the adjacent Sinnington Hall. Jane enjoys sharing her home with guests and offers three bedrooms to visitors. A large twin-bedded room has a spacious bathroom separated from the bedroom by a curtained archway. Overlooking the garden and enjoying valley views, the second bedroom has its bathroom across the hall, while a snug attic room has a tiny en-suite bathroom and adjacent sleeping area for children. Lovely flower arrangements add to the beautiful dining, sitting, and morning room where guests enjoy breakfast and the magnificent views across the valley to the distant Howard Hills and York. Sinnington lies on the edge of the North Yorkshire Moors National Park with its vast open spaces and little villages in sheltered valleys. The area is rich in historical sites—the ruined abbey of Rievaulx, the castle at Helmsley, and the stately homes of Castle Howard and Duncombe Park. The medieval city of York is half-an-hour's drive away. *Directions:* From Pickering take the A170 (signposted Helmsley) for 4 miles to Sinnington. Turn into the village, cross the green, keeping the village hall (which stands on the green) to your right, turn first right and follow the lane up the hill, bearing right by the church along a farm track that dead-ends at Hunters Hill.

HUNTERS HILL
Owners: Jane Orr
Sinnington
York Y06 6SF, England
Tel: (01751) 431196, Fax: (01751) 432976
Email: jorr@btclick.com
3 rooms
£25 per person, dinner £23.50
Open all year, Credit cards: none
Children over 12
www.karenbrown.com/england/huntershill.html

Gardening is Jane Baldwin's passion—not only does she tend her own 2 acres of exquisite gardens, but she also organizes the National Gardens Scheme in North Yorkshire and can recommend and arrange for you to visit other lovely gardens in the area. Her late-18th-century home is large enough to provide privacy for visitors and family. Guests have their own wing with a dining room (breakfast is the only meal served) and a low-ceilinged, very comfortable sitting room. A double-bedded room has a small en-suite shower room while a more spacious twin-bedded room shares a bathroom with another small single bedroom. Jane always ensures that the bathroom is never shared by guests who are not traveling together. For dinner, guests often wander by the river and across the green to the village pub—if you want to go farther afield, Jane is happy to make recommendations. Sinnington is a lovely, very quiet village just off the main Pickering to Helmsley road, an ideal base for exploring the lovely scenery and villages of the North Yorkshire Moors and making a day trip to the coast to Staithes, Robin Hood's Bay, and Whitby with its impressive abbey ruins. If you're a stately homes person, be sure to visit nearby Castle Howard and Nunnington Hall. *Directions:* From Pickering take the A170 (signposted Helmsley) for 4 miles to Sinnington. Turn into the village, cross the river, and turn right into the lane that leads to Riverside Farm.

RIVERSIDE FARM
Owners: Jane & Bill Baldwin
Sinnington
York Y062 6RY, England
Tel & fax: (01751) 431764
Email:whbaldwin@yahoo.co.uk
3 rooms
£25 per person
Open Apr to Oct, Credit cards: none
Children over 8, No-smoking house
www.karenbrown.com/riverside.html

A maze of narrow country roads connects the tiny little villages that dot the rolling countryside just to the south of Shrewsbury. Here you find Lawley House among the cluster of homes that makes up the hamlet of Smethcott. Set atop a hill, this spacious Victorian home faces glorious countryside across a lovely garden full of old-fashioned scented roses. Jackie loves welcoming guests to her home and makes sure that they are well taken care of. Relax in the spacious sitting room and adjacent conservatory that overlooks the garden and the distant Stretton Hills. The bedrooms enjoy the same lovely view. One has its bathroom en suite while the other has its spacious bathroom just across the hall. Breakfast is the only meal served round the dining-room table and for dinner guests often go to The Bottle and Glass, just down the lane in Picklescott, or to The Pound, a thatched pub in nearby Leebotwood. Walkers head for the Long Mynd and often take the one-hour walk that Jackie has outlined from the house. Shrewsbury—with its winding lanes, the castle, its many museums, the market square, and its decorative black-and-white houses—is a "must visit." Farther afield lie Powys Castle and the industrial heritage museums of Ironbridge Gorge. *Directions:* From Shrewsbury take the A49 south. At Leebotwood turn right to Smethcott and Walkmills. Follow signs uphill towards Smethcott and after 1½ miles Lawley House's drive is on your left. (Smethcott is very near Picklescott.)

LAWLEY HOUSE
Owners: Jackie & Jim Scarratt
Smethcott, near Church Stretton
Shropshire SY6 6NX, England
Tel: (01694) 751236, Fax: (01694) 751396
2 rooms
£25–£30 per person
Open all year, Credit cards: none
Children over 12, No-smoking house

Because of its close proximity to The Potteries and Leek, Rose Cottage, home to Cynthia and Peter Moore, is an ideal countryside base for shopping for fine china and antique pine. It really is the most quintessentially countryside spot—a darling cottage set on a quiet country lane just up the road from Snelston, a very pretty village. The term "cottage" conjures up visions of a modest-sized house but though Rose Cottage has its origins in a small residence, it has been expanded over the years into a substantial house of great character. Toast your toes by the fire in the snug little parlor or spread out in the spacious sitting room with its large windows framing panoramic countryside views. The same lovely view is enjoyed by the bedrooms, the largest of which also offers bucolic views from its bathroom. One bedroom has its private bathroom across the hall. Breakfast is the only meal served. Nearby Ashbourne has some excellent restaurants but we preferred the "real ale," excellent food, and old-world pub atmosphere of the Coach and Horses in the neighboring village of Fenny Bentley. Just down the road is Ashbourne with its splendid church and antique salesrooms and to the north lie the Derbyshire Dales with their magnificent scenery and beautiful walks. *Directions:* From Ashbourne take the A515 towards Lichfield. After 3 miles turn right on the B5033 in the direction of Norbury. Take the second lane to the right towards Snelston and Rose Cottage is the second house on the right behind a tall beech hedge.

ROSE COTTAGE   **New**
Owners: Cynthia & Peter Moore
Snelston, Ashbourne
Derbyshire DE6 2DL, England
Tel: (01335) 324230, Fax: (01335) 324651
Email: pjmoore@beeb.net
3 rooms
£25–£27 per person
Closed Christmas, Credit cards: none
Children over 12, No-smoking house
www.karenbrown.com/england/rosecottage.html

The Lynch Country House was built for an attorney and his bride in 1812 and was owned by their family for over a hundred years. Roy Copeland purchased the house with the intention of running a country house hotel: however, when the renovations were complete he decided that a bed and breakfast was more his cup of tea. Consequently guests get country-house-style accommodation at bed-and-breakfast prices. Roy encourages guests to enjoy the lovely gardens with their topiary hedges and lake with its resident family of black swans. Bedrooms vary in size from snug rooms under the eaves (Alderley is an especially attractive attic room) to Goldington, a large high-ceilinged room with a grand Georgian four-poster bed. Roy supplies a list of restaurants and pubs in each room along with sample menus but finds that guests usually stroll into the village to The Globe pub. Somerton, long ago the capital of Wessex, is now a substantial village with some interesting shops and pretty streets lined with old stone houses. Glastonbury, the cradle of English Christianity, and Wells with its magnificent cathedral are nearby. Bath is just under an hour away. *Directions:* From the Podimore roundabout on the A303 follow signposts for Langport and Somerton. Join the A372 and turn right after a mile for Somerton. Ignore the next two Somerton signs and take the third left by the dairy. Lynch Country House is at the top of the hill by the mini roundabout.

THE LYNCH COUNTRY HOUSE
Owner: Roy Copeland
4 Behind Berry, Somerton
Somerset TA11 7PD, England
Tel: (01458) 272316, Fax: (01458) 272590
Email: the_lynch@talk21.com
5 rooms
£24.50–£42.50 per person
Closed Christmas & New Year, Credit cards: all major
Children over 16
www.karenbrown.com/england/thelynchcountryhouse.html

People enjoy themselves at Sproxton Hall—they relax, they unwind, and they simply enjoy the warm hospitality of this comfortable 17th-century farmhouse on its 300 acres of land. Relax round the fire in the beamed drawing room and enjoy the heartiest of breakfasts in the dining room. For dinner Margaret will direct you to comfortable country pubs in local villages. The flowery bedrooms are delightfully color-coordinated and have country views. The blue room has a double bed, brass bedhead, and swathes of fabric to create a half-tester and is accompanied by an en-suite shower room. Another double room has its private bathroom across the hallway. The end of the hallway is curtained off to provide a suite of rooms with a double, a twin, and a bathroom—this is only ever let to one party. A mile up the road is the pretty market town of Helmsley with its interesting shops set round the cobbled market square. Medieval York lies 21 miles to the south. Take your pick of nearby stately homes (Nunnington Hall, Castle Howard) and abbeys (Byland, Rievaulx) and head farther afield to Robin Hood's Bay and the fishing port of Whitby. *Directions:* Helmsley is on the A170 between Thirsk and Pickering. One mile south of Helmsley take the B1257 towards Malton and turn left beside the church, following the lane to the end where you find Sproxton Hall.

SPROXTON HALL
Owners: Margaret & Andrew Wainwright
Sproxton
Helmsley
North Yorkshire YO62 5EQ, England
Tel: (01439) 770225, Fax: (01439) 771373
3 rooms
£24–£28 per person
Closed Christmas & New Year, Credit cards: MC, VS
Children over 10

The food at The Angel Inn is outstanding and, fortunately for visitors to this pretty part of Suffolk, guests may lodge as well as dine here. When the inn was purchased in 1985, it was in a sorry state, but now its complete refurbishment has transformed it into a building with lots of charm and old-world ambiance. Guests eating in the bar make their selection from the menu hung on the old red-brick wall above the fireplace and then settle down at one of the tables grouped under the low, beamed ceiling. (It is best to avoid the crush by arriving early or just before last orders at 9 pm.) Those who prefer a quieter, no-smoking atmosphere may elect to eat in the dramatic 16th-century hall with its lofty rafters where tables are laid with linen and soft lighting adds a romantic mood. Wherever you dine you have the identical choice of tempting fare. Bedrooms are pleasantly furnished and have a light, airy decor. Room 6 with its high, beamed ceiling is the premier room. Please be aware that you can hear the sounds from the bar in the bedrooms. This unspoilt region of quiet countryside offers lots of sightseeing, such as the nearby valley of the River Stour, Dedham, and Flatford Mill, all made famous by John Constable's paintings. *Directions:* Take the A134 Sudbury road from Colchester for 5 miles to Nayland, then turn right for the 2-mile drive to Stoke by Nayland.

THE ANGEL INN
Manager: Mike Everett
Stoke by Nayland
Colchester
Essex CO6 4SA, England
Tel: (01206) 263245, Fax: (01206) 263373
6 rooms
£34 per person, dinner £15–£20
Closed Christmas, Credit cards: MC, VS
Children over 10

A few minutes' walk from the busy village of Storrington, in the heart of the historic South Downs, Lime Chase is a modern house modeled in traditional Sussex style. Down a private drive and set in an immaculately tended garden, it provides the traveler with a welcome cocoon of hospitality. Guests arriving in the afternoon are welcomed with tea and freshly baked scones served in the spacious conservatory or on the patio in summer, by a bright log fire in the lounge on colder days. The house is beautifully decorated and furnished with antiques and collectibles that tell of the Wartons' own travels around the world. There are two spacious and extremely comfortable double bedrooms. My favorite was the ground-floor Queen Anne room, with furnishings to match the name and a luxuriously appointed en-suite bathroom. The first-floor room has an equally, if not more, luxurious private bathroom next door and can be supplemented with another double room downstairs. Guests gather for a sumptuous breakfast around the large table in the dining room, sharing their plans for the day ahead. Local attractions include Petworth House with its Turner paintings, the Weald and Downland Museum of Rural Life, and Arundel Castle. *Directions:* From the A24 take the A283 into Storrington and at the mini roundabout take the B2139 towards Thakenham. Pass the fire station on your right and turn left into Fryern Drive (signposted West Chittington). After about ¼ mile pass Mill Drive on the left and look for a curved white signpost marked "Lime Chase" on your right. Lime Chase is the first house on the right. (There is no sign on the house.)

LIME CHASE New
Owners: Fiona & Keith Warton
1 Lime Chase, Storrington
West Sussex RH20 4LX, England
Tel & fax: (01903) 740437
Email: fionawarton@limechase.com
2 rooms
£35–£45 per person
Open all year, Credit cards: none
Children over 12, No-smoking house
www.karenbrown.com/england/limechase.html

Just a few minutes' walk from town, this square, three-story building with rich salmon-colored façade and white trim stands out amongst the many row houses offering bed and breakfast accommodation. Although we discovered the delightful, family-run Caterham House Hotel not long ago, it has existed under the same proprietorship for 25 years and the register boasts a majority of loyal returning guests. With the owners being originally from France, this hotel has a charming, subtly French influence both in its decor and ambiance. Soft tones of yellow and mauve dominate the color scheme and creative touches such as attractive stenciling, interesting art, and a beautiful quilt hung as a headboard make each room refreshing and unique. Off the entry there is a welcoming sitting room with full bar and outside terrace for guests to enjoy. To accommodate the ten guestrooms in the main building, Dominique and Olive cleverly took down the shared wall of two adjoining buildings, so when you climb the interior stairs it seems almost an illusion as an apparently mirrored staircase rises up to meet the other. A renovated neighboring cottage houses two additional rooms. Although there is no restaurant, Dominique tailors breakfast to whatever guests want, be it traditional English with eggs and sausage or French with croissants and coffee. *Directions:* Turn left at the American Fountain coming from the town center, and right coming from the train station, into Rother Street. The Caterham House Hotel is on the left just past the police station.

CATERHAM HOUSE HOTEL
Owners: Olive & Dominique Maury
58/59 Rother Street
Stratford-upon-Avon
Warwickshire CV37 6LT, England
Tel: (01789) 267309, Fax: (01789) 414836
12 rooms
£40–£45 per person
Open all year, Credit cards: MC, VS
Children welcome
www.karenbrown.com/england/caterham.html

Home to Stella and Eddie Davies, their two children, and dog Maisie, The Crofts Farm house stands beside the 280-acre arable farm for which it is named. Eddie operates the farm and provides the hard labor to support Stella's landscaping plans for their nearly 2 acres of gardens, which include a well-manicured grass court for the use of resident tennis aficionados. The house is a red-bricked Georgian affair dating back to the 1750s, revamped and updated in the pre-Victorian 1800s, with large rooms and tall windows. A curved staircase leads up from the flagstone entrance hall to the three comfortable bedrooms (two double and one family) with their mix of en-suite or private bathrooms. A sitting room downstairs provides a snug haven on gloomy days and full farmhouse breakfasts are served in the dining room. A five-minute drive finds you in the bustle of Stratford town center, which, despite the large number of sightseers, manages to keep its beauty. You can visit Shakespeare's likely birthplace in Henley Street, the schoolroom in the guildhall where he learned his first lessons, an Elizabethan knot garden near the foundations of New Place where he died, and his wife Anne Hathaway's cottage. Try to catch one of his plays performed at the Royal Shakespeare Theatre and the newer theater, The Other Place. Also wander into Warwick, with its mixture of Georgian and old timber houses and magnificent castle. *Directions:* The Crofts Farm is down a private driveway on the east side of the A422 about 2 miles south of Stratford.

THE CROFTS FARM   New
Owners: Stella & Eddie Davies
Banbury Road, Stratford-upon-Avon
Warwickshire CV37 7NF, England
Tel: (01789) 292159, Fax: none
Email: edstell@croftsfarm.freeserve.co.uk
3 rooms
£28–£35 per person
Open Easter to Oct, Credit cards: MC, VS
Children welcome, No-smoking house
www.karenbrown.com/england/croftsfarm.html

Bed & Breakfast Descriptions

Thomas Luny, the marine artist, had this home built in 1792 in the center of Teignmouth, just a short walk through narrow streets from the sheltered harbor, which has a long history as a fishing and ship-building center. Now this handsome house is home to Alison and John Allan and their two children. All the rooms have an en-suite bathroom, a television, mineral water, and a lovely old sea chest. Each is decorated in a contrasting style: Chinese enjoys a peach-and-green decor and painted Oriental furniture; Clairmont is pretty in green and yellow; Luny is autumnal in beige and brown; and Bitton contemporary with its impressive four-poster bed. A scrumptious breakfast is the only meal served but there is no shortage of eating places a few minutes' walk or a short drive away. Follow the narrow streets of old Teignmouth to the working harbor and along to the Victorian section of town with its long sandy beach, cheerful pier, and esplanade popular with the bucket-and-spade brigade. Just across the estuary lies Shaldon where every Wednesday, from May to September, residents dress in 18th-century costume. *Directions:* From Exeter take the A380 towards Torquay for 3 miles to the B3192 to Teignmouth. Turn left at the traffic lights at the bottom of the hill, then turn immediately right at next set of traffic lights, signposted Quays, and immediately left into Teign Street. Thomas Luny House is on your right.

THOMAS LUNY HOUSE
Owners: Alison & John Allan
Teign Street
Teignmouth
Devon TQ14 8EG, England
Tel: (01626) 772976, Fax: none
Email: alisonandjohn@thomas-luny-house.co.uk
4 rooms
£37.50 per person
Open all year, Credit cards: MC, VS
Children over 12
www.karenbrown.com/england/thomasluny.html

Dale Head Hall occupies a stunning, isolated position on the shores of Thirlmere, one of Cumbria's quietest, most pastoral lakes, and provides the perfect base for exploring the entire Lake District. Front bedrooms offer gorgeous lake views while the delightful rooms at the back in the old part of the house are low-ceilinged with old latch doors and beams. One of the back bedrooms has a small cradle room snug above the inglenook fireplace. Two lake-view rooms on the ground floor are handy for those who have a problem with stairs. I particularly like the ground-floor twin with its private lake-facing patio and own entrance patio with chairs. Superior rooms are rented only on a dinner, bed, and breakfast basis. Much of the lovely oak furniture found throughout the hotel is the handiwork of personable Alan Lowe who joins his wife Shirley, daughter Caroline, and son-in-law Hans in making certain that guests are well taken care of and well fed. Walks from the hotel range from a stroll around the lake to challenging hikes up the nearby fells. For a week's stay, Dale Head Hall has several delightful apartments in the adjacent stables. *Directions:* Leave the M6 at junction 40 and take the A66 towards Keswick then the B5322 signposted Windermere to join the A591, which you take in the direction of Windermere for ½ mile. The entrance to Dale Head Hall is on your right.

DALE HEAD HALL
Owners: Shirley & Alan Lowe,
  Caroline & Hans Bonkenburg
Lake Thirlmere, Keswick
Cumbria CA12 4TN, England
Tel: (017687) 72478, Fax: (017687) 71070
Email: onthelakeside@dale-head-hall.co.uk
12 rooms, 7 apartments
£35–£55 per person, dinner £30
Superior room £90–£95 per person*
*Dinner, bed & breakfast
Open Feb to Dec, Credit cards: all major
Children welcome
www.karenbrown.com/ews/daleheadhall.html

Standing in over an acre of carefully tended gardens and surrounded by parkland, Spital Hill provides a tranquil retreat just a ten-minute drive from the busy A1. The house is of Georgian origin, with Victorian additions. Hosts Ann and Robin Clough have named the three large and comfortably furnished bedrooms after family relatives and friends. Emmie has a queen-size double bed, Muriel has two full-size twins, and Anthony is equipped with not only a large double bed but also its own piano, which guests are actively encouraged to play. All have ample en-suite bathrooms. The house is furnished throughout with family heirlooms and antiques. Robin entertains guests with pre-dinner drinks in the sitting room while Ann applies the meal's finishing touches in the kitchen, using fresh produce from the garden. A hand-picked wine list complements the food. Just up the road, shops overlook Thirsk's cobbled market square. Here you can visit the Herriot Centre, the former veterinary surgery of James Herriot, quiet local vet-turned-author. Nearby villages include Kilburn and Coxwold, the former associated with the "mouse man" and his oak furniture and the latter famous for Shandy Hall, the home of Laurence Sterne. There is an amazing view from nearby Sutton Bank. York, Castle Howard, and the Yorkshire Moors all make excellent day trips. *Directions:* Spital Hill is 1 mile south of the A19 (A170)/168 junction on the A19, Thirsk to York road. The entrance to Spital Hill is marked by two short white posts at the roadside.

SPITAL HILL　　New
Owners: Ann & Robin Clough
Thirsk
North Yorkshire Y07 3AE, England
Tel: (01845) 522273, Fax: (01845) 524970
3 rooms
£33–£45 per person, dinner £28
Open all year, Credit cards: all major
Children over 12, No-smoking house
www.karenbrown.com/england/spital.html

Nether Hall's garden is so lovely that it should be declared an area of outstanding beauty, particularly when the roses that envelop the old barn, cascade from the trees, and clamber across the house are in bloom. In amidst the landscaping you find a hard tennis court, a 400-year-old pond, and the gently meandering River Box. Inside Nether Hall, Jennie and Patrick Jackson's home, all is equally delightful. Guests have lots of privacy in a suite of rooms just for them. Here you find a dining room (only breakfast served) with the polished table set before an enormous inglenook fireplace and an adjacent sitting room full of comfortable chairs. Just off the dining room is the most beautiful of bedrooms with a private entrance to the garden and zip and link (king or twin) beds set beneath a beamed ceiling. Upstairs are two more bedrooms—an en-suite double and a smaller twin-bedded room with its adorable little bathroom across the hall. Here you are in the heart of Constable country where John Constable worked—the mill and nearby Will Lott's cottage at Flatford Mill are much as he painted them. The area has some delightfully picturesque villages. *Directions:* Thorington Street is 3 miles from the A12 on the B1068 between the villages of Higham and Stoke by Nayland. Arriving from Higham, Nether Hall is on your left just before you come to Thorington Street.

NETHER HALL
Owners: Jennie & Patrick Jackson
Thorington Street, Stoke by Nayland
Suffolk CO6 45T, England
Tel: (01206) 337373, Fax: (01206) 337496
Email: patrick.jackson@talk21.com
3 rooms
£30 per person
Open all year, Credit cards: none
Children over 12, No-smoking house
www.karenbrown.com/england/nether.html

Claiming the honor of being King Arthur's legendary birthplace, the ruins of Tintagel Castle cling to a wild headland exposed to the coastal winds. It's a place of myths that attracts visitors who come to soak up its fanciful past and enjoy its rugged scenery. While the village of Tintagel is a touristy spot, just a mile away lies the quiet hamlet of Trenale, a cluster of cottages, and the delightful Trebrea Lodge. Behind the impressive, tall Georgian façade lies a much older building of cozy, comfortable rooms. Upstairs, the drawing room is full of splendid antiques but you will probably find yourself downstairs toasting your toes by the fire enveloped by a large armchair, enjoying drinks and coffee after one of Sean's delicious, award-winning dinners in the paneled dining room with its views across stone-walled fields to the distant sea. We particularly enjoyed our room (4) furnished, as are all the rooms, with lovely antiques and enjoying a large bathroom; the four-poster room (1) with its ornately carved Victorian four-poster bed; and room 5, a delightful twin-bedded room with its view to the distant ocean. A tempting array of hot breakfast dishes is placed on the buffet for guests to help themselves. Walkers enjoy spectacular cliff-top walks along rugged headlands. To the north lies Clovelly. *Directions:* From Tintagel take the road towards Boscastle and at the edge of Tintagel turn right at the contemporary-style Roman Catholic church. Turn right at the top of the lane and Trebrea Lodge is on your left.

TREBREA LODGE
Owners: John Charlick & Sean Devlin
Trenale, Tintagel
Cornwall PL34 0HR, England
Tel: (01840) 770410, Fax: (01840) 770092
Email: trebrea-lodge@supernet.com
7 rooms
£43–£48 per person, dinner £24.50
Open mid-Feb to mid-Dec, Credit cards: all major
Children over 12
www.karenbrown.com/england/trebrealodge.html

Patsy and Richard Mason transformed a tumbledown cottage and barn in an overgrown field by a stream into a delightful home facing a lake in an idyllic 6-acre garden complete with stream and many unusual plants and shrubs. The house is just as attractive inside as out. Sofas are drawn up around the wood-burning stove in the beamed sitting room. In addition to a double room on the ground floor the accommodation consists of two more, very nicely furnished bedrooms upstairs. All rooms have extremely powerful showers in newly equipped shower rooms. During the warm summer months, evening barbecues may be served on the terrace or in the conservatory (with prior notice). There are many alternative local eating places. One of Patsy's suggested day trips takes in the National Rose Collection at Mottisfont Abbey, Hilliers Arboretum, and finally Broadlands, the home of the late Lord Mountbatten. Salisbury, Winchester, and Stonehenge are all 15 miles distant. Other services include airport collection from Heathrow and Gatwick with car hire delivered to Malt Cottage and trout fishing on one of the many local waters, including the famous River Test. *Directions:* From the A303, at Andover, take the A3057 (towards Stockbridge) and turn first right, signposted for Upper Clatford. Take the first left, go right at the T-junction, and turn right opposite the Crook and Shears pub into a little lane leading to Malt Cottage.

MALT COTTAGE
Owners: Patsy & Richard Mason
Upper Clatford
Andover
Hampshire SP11 7QL, England
Tel: (01264) 323469, Fax: (01264) 334100
Email: info@maltcottage.co.uk
3 rooms
£30–£35 per person, dinner £15
Closed Christmas & New Year, Credit cards: none
Children welcome, No-smoking house
www.karenbrown.com/england/maltcottage.html

Standing on the corner of St. John's Hill, a charming little square on the edge of the very attractive little town of Wareham, Gold Court House was built in 1762 on the foundations of a 13th-century cottage where the local goldsmith lived. Now it is the spacious, lovely home of Anthea and Michael Hipwell and, fortunately for guests, they continue to offer the same hospitable welcome (along with a tail-wagging greeting from Cedar, the labrador) as they did for over 15 years at The Old Vicarage in Affpuddle. All the spacious, well-decorated bedrooms overlook the lovely walled garden. Two are found up the main staircase, while the third has a private entry off the garden. Breakfast is the only meal served but Anthea offers advice on pubs and restaurants to walk to for dinner. Likewise, Anthea helps guests plan their exploration of Hardy country or visits to the haunts of Lawrence of Arabia. The Dorset coast (Lulworth Cove, Dirdle Door, and Ringstead Bay) is close at hand. Nearby are the historic towns of Dorchester, Sherbourne, and Poole, with lots to see and good shopping. *Directions:* Wareham is on the A351 between Poole and Swanage. Cross the River Piddle and go down North Street into South Street. As you see the River Frome in front of you, turn left into St. John's Hill. Gold Court House is on the corner.

GOLD COURT HOUSE
Owners: Anthea & Michael Hipwell
St. John's Hill
Wareham
Dorset BH20 4LZ, England
Tel & fax: (01929) 553320
3 rooms
£22.50–£25 per person, dinner £11 (winter only)
Closed Christmas to New Year, Credit cards: none
Children over 10, No-smoking house
www.karenbrown.com/england/goldcourt.html

Romney Marsh was once the haunt of smugglers who carried wool to France and brought back lace, salt, and, as Kipling said, "brandy for the parson, backy for the clerk." At the very heart of the marsh a Union Jack flies from a tall flagpole, bidding you welcome to Terry House, the lovely former farmhouse home of Adele and Peter Sherston. In the morning you will have a hearty breakfast at the pine table in the kitchen. Two bedrooms are found in the main house: a pretty double with pink sprigged wallpaper—very homey with lots of books and delightful Rye pottery animals—and a smart twin-bedded room with its private bathroom directly across the hall. However, I would opt to stay in the stable cottage across the garden. With its delightful bedroom, bathroom, and comfortable sitting room stocked with books, it offers lots of comfort and gives you privacy and the ability to really settle in and make yourself at home. The marsh is on your doorstep and footpaths take you along dykes and over canals. Medieval marsh churches are a great attraction in this area and this is a perfect location for day trips to Rye, Tunbridge Wells, and Canterbury or visits to gardens such as Great Dixter and Sissinghurst. *Directions*: Leave the M20 at exit 10 for Brenzett and take the A2070 for 6 miles. Turn right for Hamstreet and then immediately left. In Hamstreet turn right onto the B2067 then left for Warehorne Church. Go through Warehorne and Terry House is 1 mile along on your right after the level crossing.

TERRY HOUSE
Owners: Adele & Peter Sherston
Warehorne, Ashford
Kent TN26 2LS, England
Tel: (01233) 732443, Fax: (01233) 732466
Email: jsherston@ukonline.co.uk
3 rooms
£22–£30 per person
Open all year, Credit cards: none
Children welcome, No-smoking house
www.karenbrown.com/england/terryhouse.html

Wartling Place is a fine white Victorian house with Georgian origins in the heart of the Sussex countryside. It stands well back from the road in acres of grounds in the pretty village of Wartling, close to the 13th-century church. At one time Wartling Place was a rectory but now it's the home of Rowena and Barry Gittoes and their family. It's a captivating place—relaxing and happy—and large enough for guests to have lots of privacy and space. Two of the large bedrooms have antique queen-sized four-poster beds and two have brass beds. All are delightfully kitted out and accompanied by en-suite bathrooms. Breakfast is served in the spacious guest sitting/dining room. Dinner is available by prior arrangement or you can go to the Lamb Inn opposite. If you would like to stay for a week, there's a delightful two-bedroom cottage in the garden. Just up the road is Herstmonceux Castle, a romantic, fortified 15th-century house complete with moat and crusaders' tombs in the old church opposite the castle entrance. Other popular places to visit include Charleston, Virginia Wolfe's home, Bodiam Castle, quaint Rye with its cobbled streets, and the gardens at Pashley Manor and Great Dixter. *Directions:* Five miles outside Eastbourne the A22 joins the A27—at this point take the A271 towards Bexhill through Herstmonceux and turn right after Windmill Hill for Wartling. Wartling Place is just after the Lamb Inn on the right.

WARTLING PLACE
Owners: Rowena & Barry Gittoes
Wartling, Herstmonceux
East Sussex BN27 1RY, England
Tel: (01323) 832590, Fax: (01323) 831558
4 rooms, 1 cottage
£35–£49 per person, cottage to £500, dinner £25
Open all year, Credit cards: all major
Children welcome, No-smoking house

Beryl, a Gothic Revival mansion on 13 acres of grounds just a mile from Wells Cathedral, is a grand house full of lovely antiques and home to Holly and Eddie Nowell and their family—a home they enjoy sharing with visitors. The measure of their success is the large number of returning guests who bring their family, friends, and even dogs (provided that they are compatible with the resident chocolate lab). Lovers of elegant antiques will delight in those found in every nook and cranny of the house—Eddie is a well-known antique dealer. All the bedrooms have special features. We loved our attic room, Summer, all pretty in pink and white with daisies on the wallpaper and bedcovers. Next door, Spring has an elegantly draped four-poster bed to leap (literally) into. Principal bedrooms are larger and grander—choose Winston if you have a passion for grand, old-fashioned, climb-into bathtubs, Butterfly if you enjoy space and want to wake up with Wells Cathedral framed in the enormous bay window. Chair-lift access is available to the main floor of bedrooms. Wells is England's smallest city, with the most glorious cathedral. *Directions:* Leave or approach Wells on the B3139 in the direction of The Horringtons. Turn into Hawkers Lane opposite the Shell garage. Drive to the top of the lane and continue straight into Beryl's driveway.

BERYL
Owners: Holly & Eddie Nowell
Hawkers Lane
Wells
Somerset BA5 3JP, England
Tel: (01749) 678738, Fax: (01749) 670508
Email: stay@beryl-wells.co.uk
7 rooms
£37.50–£47.50 per person, dinner £22.50 (not Sun)
Closed Christmas, Credit cards: MC, VS
Children welcome
www.karenbrown.com/england/beryl.html

The Citadel sits like a mighty fortress on a knoll overlooking verdant countryside. As soon as you cross the threshold, you realize this is not a "castle" of drafty halls and stone chambers, but a lovely home built to a fanciful design. A spacious sitting room occupies one of the turrets and leads to the large billiard room. You are welcome to bring your own wine to accompany supper in the dining room. Up the broad staircase, two of the bedrooms occupy turrets. Each has an adjacent Victorian-style bathroom with claw-foot tub center stage. A lovely twin-bedded room has an en-suite shower room. As an added bonus there are 3 acres of glorious gardens to admire. The adjacent golf club is a popular venue, but the real magic of the area lies in a visit to Hawkstone Park where you follow an intricate network of pathways through woodlands and across a narrow log bridge to high cliffs, a ruined castle, mystical grotto, and giant obelisk. The Ironbridge Gorge Museums, Shrewsbury, and Chester are within an hour's drive. *Directions:* From Shrewsbury, take the A49 (north) for 12 miles, turn right for Hodnet and Weston-under-Redcastle, and The Citadel is on your right, a quarter of a mile after leaving Weston-under-Redcastle (before Hawkstone Park).

THE CITADEL
Owners: Sylvia & Beverley Griffiths
Weston-under-Redcastle
Shrewsbury
Shropshire SY4 5JY, England
Tel & fax: (01630) 685204
Email: griffiths@citadel2000.freeserve.co.uk
3 rooms
£45 per person, dinner £20 (not Sun)
Open Apr to Oct, Credit cards: none
Children over 12, No-smoking house
www.karenbrown.com/england/citadel.html

Built for the High Sheriff of Shropshire in 1690, Dearnford Hall has been the Bebbington family home for three generations. Now that their three children have grown up and flown the nest, Jane enjoys looking after her guests while her husband Chas is busy running their 500-acre arable farm. The atmosphere is relaxed and friendly, and the decor is delightful. The large bedrooms are bright and sunny, with rich fabrics, deep mattresses, fat duvets, and fine linen, while the sparkling modern bathrooms boast power showers and baths. After a hearty English breakfast served in the dining room, you can explore walled Chester, perfect for browsing in antique stores, or Shrewsbury, following in the steps of Brother Cadfael, the medieval sleuthing monk. Snowdonia, The Potteries, Ironbridge, and a wealth of National Trust houses at Erddig, Powis, and Chirk are all within easy reach. You can visit famous local gardens at reduced prices with one of Jane's Great Gardens Passports. Wander through the farm to the trout lake—Molly, their flat-coat retriever, will show you the way. Jane can arrange fly-fishing tuition and rod hire. Jane recommends a variety of excellent restaurants or pubs for an evening meal. Feel free to play the Steinway in the hall or relax by a log fire in the evening to round off your day. *Directions:* From Whitchurch bypass take the B5476 towards Tilstock and Wem for half a mile and Dearnford Hall is the second farm on the left-hand side.

DEARNFORD HALL
Owners: Jane & Chas Bebbington
Whitchurch,
Shropshire SY13 3JJ, England
Tel: (01948) 662319, Fax: (01948) 666670
Email: dearnford_hall@yahoo.com
2 rooms
£38–£50 per person
Closed Christmas, Credit cards: MC, VS
Children over 15, No-smoking house
www.karenbrown.com/england/dearnford.html

Stratford-upon-Avon is a Mecca for visitors who come for everything associated with Shakespeare: the performances of his plays, the town's Tudor buildings, Anne Hathaway's cottage, and Mary Arden's house. Just across the garden from Mary Arden's house you find Pear Tree Cottage, home to Margaret and Ted Mander for almost forty years, a home that has been sympathetically extended to provide seven en-suite bedrooms for guests. All the rooms are delightful, though I particularly enjoyed those in the old cottage simply because they have an especially old-world feeling. Guests have an attractive small sitting room and breakfast room with little tables and chairs set in front of a dresser displaying decorative blue-and-white plates. Two modern kitchens are available for guests to prepare their picnics or suppers. Margaret and Ted really look after guests, providing them with an excellent map of Stratford that highlights all the things to see and, most importantly, indicates where to conveniently park your car when sightseeing or going to the theater (they can help guests to obtain tickets). Another map outlines a day tour through Cotswold villages, highlighting all the gardens, villages, houses and pubs. *Directions:* From Stratford-upon-Avon take the A3400 signposted for Henley-in-Arden for 2½ miles. Turn left to Wilmcote and Pear Tree Cottage is in the center of the village.

PEAR TREE COTTAGE
Owners: Margaret & Ted Mander
Church Road, Wilmcote
Stratford-upon-Avon
Warwickshire CV37 9UX, England
Tel: (01789) 205889, Fax: (01789) 262862
Email: mander@peartreecot.co.uk
7 rooms
£27–£29 per person
Open Feb to Dec, Credit cards: none
Children over 3, No-smoking house
www.karenbrown.com/england/peartreecottage.html

Nestled beside the baby River Isbourne on a quiet county lane just a few yards from the main street of the delightfully pretty Cotswold village of Winchcombe, Isbourne Manor House dates back to Elizabethan times, with extensive Georgian additions. From the moment you enter, you will be delighted by the attractive decor and warmth of hospitality offered by Felicity and David King. The elegant drawing room with its wood-burning fire is exclusively for guests' use. Breakfast is the only meal served in the dining room, but the Kings provide an extensive list of suggested eating places in the area. Splurge and request The Sudeley Room, well worth the few additional pounds to enjoy its elegant queen-sized four-poster bed swathed with peach-colored draperies. Langley is a most attractive double-bedded room decorated in shades of cream. Under the steeply sloping eaves of the Elizabethan portion of the house you find the snug quarters offered by Beesmore whose window serves as the door onto a large rooftop terrace. Beesmore's bathroom is down the hall. Walk to nearby Sudeley Castle, more of a stately home than a traditional castle, then set out on a day-long tour of Cotswold villages with Bourton-on-the-Water, Stow-on-the-Wold, Chipping Campden, and Broadway being popular destinations. *Directions:* Winchcombe is on the B4632 between Cheltenham and Broadway. Turn into Castle Street (in the center of the village) and Isbourne Manor House is on the left just before the little bridge.

ISBOURNE MANOR HOUSE
Owners: Felicity & David King
Castle Street, Winchcombe
Gloucestershire GL54 6JA, England
Tel & fax: (01242) 602281
Email: felicity@isbourne-manor.co.uk
3 rooms
£27.50–£40 per person
Open all year, Credit cards: none
Children over 10, No-smoking house
www.karenbrown.com/england/isbournemanorhouse.html

Sudeley Lodge, built in 1760 as a grand home on the Sudeley Castle estate, sits high on a hill overlooking rolling countryside beyond its acres of gorgeous gardens. Jim grew up here and when his parents found the house too big for them, they divided it into two with Jim, Susie, and their family having the Westward wing. Susie welcomes guests with tea and cake, encouraging them to make themselves at home in the drawing room, wander round the gardens, and walk on the farm. Upstairs, the spacious bedrooms have lovely views across the garden to the countryside. Susie loves to cook and candlelit dinners are sometimes available. There is no shortage of excellent places to eat both in nearby Winchcombe and the surrounding villages. Just down the road is Sudeley Castle with its parklike setting, magnificent medieval exterior, and largely Victorianized interior. This is an ideal spot for exploring a plethora of Cotswold villages such as Broadway, Snowshill, Chipping Campden, Lower Slaughter, and Stow-on-the-Wold. *Directions:* Winchcombe is on the B4632 between Cheltenham and Broadway. Turn into Castle Street (in the center of the village) and proceed up the hill. Pass the farm buildings on the right and turn right, signed for Sudeley Lodge. Pass two cottages on the way to the house.

WESTWARD AT SUDELEY LODGE
Owners: Susie & Jim Wilson
Winchcombe
Gloucestershire GL54 5JB, England
Tel: (01242) 604372, Fax: (01242) 604640
Email: jimw@haldon.co.uk
3 rooms
£35–£42.50 per person, dinner £22.50
Closed Christmas & New Year, Credit cards: MC, VS
Children over 12
www.karenbrown.com/england/westwardatsudeley.html

Just beside the cathedral in a maze of little streets in the oldest part of Winchester, you can find comfortable accommodation at The Wykeham Arms and, across the road, under the same ownership, at The Saint George. The 250-year-old Wykeham Arms is an extraordinarily convivial and welcoming inn, with log fires, candles, over 600 pictures on the walls, 1,500 tankards hanging from beams, walls, and windows, and masses of Winchester College memorabilia. In the pub food ranges from elaborate to tasty, traditional fare, while a more sophisticated menu is offered at quieter tables in the Bishop's Bar or the Watchmaker's Room. Refurbishment of bedrooms upstairs, each with a different theme, will be complete by mid-2002. I loved Hamilton, a twin with red walls above white paneling, dozens of pictures of royalty and all things military, and a huge bathroom with brick fireplace. The Saint George was converted from two tiny row houses and has the quaint attraction of a post office and shop just off the parlor. Up the narrow staircase there are four large, immaculate bedrooms, with absolutely everything from a sumptuous bathroom to a fax or modem point, and a snug single. Offering most space is the Old College Bakehouse, a little cottage in the garden, with a large sitting room and bathroom downstairs, bedroom upstairs, and tall arched, leaded windows opening up to rooftop views. *Directions:* Winchester is between junctions 9 and 10 on the M3. The hotel is located near the cathedral—Peter will send you a map so that you can navigate through the pedestrian zone to the pub's car park.

THE WYKEHAM ARMS & THE SAINT GEORGE
Managers: Kate & Peter Miller
75 Kingsgate Street
Winchester, Hampshire SO23 9PD, England
Tel: (01962) 853834, Fax: (01962) 854411
Email: doreen@wykehamarms.fsnet.co.uk
12 rooms
£40–£65 per person, dinner £22.50 (average)
Closed Christmas Day, Credit cards: all major
Children over 14
www.karenbrown.com/england/wykehamarms.html

Just 5 miles from the Georgian splendors of Bath, Burghope Manor is the 13th-century home of Liz and John Denning. Much of the present house dates from Tudor times and Burghope has strong associations with Henry VIII's prelate Archbishop Cranmer. Liz is a vivacious person who loves meeting people from all walks of life and all over the world and enjoys sharing her lovely home with them. Guests are encouraged to make themselves at home in the large pink drawing room, though they often prefer the cozier confines of the morning room. Upstairs, the spacious, lovely bedrooms, all equipped with color TV and tea- and coffee-making facilities, are each accompanied by an en-suite bathroom with bath and shower. For dinner, guests stroll into Winsley village to dine at the Seven Stars pub or Nightingales restaurant. If you are planning on staying a week or more, consider renting the Dower House, a luxurious three-bed, three-bath home sitting in the grounds. There are enough activities in Bath and nearby Bradford on Avon to occupy a week. *Directions:* From Bath take the A36 towards Warminster for 5 miles and turn left on the B3108 signposted Winsley and Bradford on Avon. Follow the road up the hill to Winsley, at the start of the bypass take the first right into the village, then at the mini crossroads turn left. The manor's front gates are at the top of the lane.

BURGHOPE MANOR
Owners: Liz & John Denning
Winsley
Bradford on Avon
Wiltshire BA15 LA, England
Tel: (01225) 723557, Fax: (01225) 723113
Email: burghope.manor@virgin.net
8 rooms
£42.50–£50 per person, dinner for groups only
Closed Christmas & New Year, Credit cards: all major
Children over 10, No-smoking house
www.karenbrown.com/england/burghopemanor.html

The Old Wharf's idyllic setting provides an entrancing first impression. A lane leading off the main highway wends its way down to a delightful small building hugging the edge of a tiny canal. Nearby, cows graze peacefully in meadows that stretch as far as the eye can see. The enclosed front patio is ablaze with a riot of color: a luxuriant cottage garden of colorful flowers, beautifully manicured yet artfully exuberant. The side of the house that opens onto the meandering stream is laced with climbing white roses. The spell of the initial impression remains unbroken when you go inside. Moira and David have taken an old warehouse and converted it into their home, incorporating an outstanding small bed and breakfast. The decor throughout is fresh and airy and extremely pretty. Moira has managed to cleverly combine lovely pastel fabrics with natural-wood-finish antiques to achieve a very pretty country look. Primrose has a small double-bedded bedroom and a snug sitting room with tall windows opening up to views of the river and fields. Breakfast is the only meal served. Within easy reach are the towns of the Sussex coast, Petworth House, and Arundel Castle. *Directions:* From Billingshurst take the A272 towards Petworth, cross the canal and river, and The Old Wharf is 50 yards after the river on the left.

THE OLD WHARF
Owners: Moira & David Mitchell
Wisborough Green
Billingshurst
Sussex RH14 OJG, England
Tel & fax: (01403) 784096
3 rooms
£37.50–£45 per person
Closed Dec 15 to Jan 6, Credit cards: none
Children over 12, No-smoking house

Shirkoak Farm is a superb place to hide away with someone you love. It's in the beautiful Weald of Kent, a lush, green land of gently undulating countryside patterned with fruit orchards, green pastures with plump sheep, cornfields, woodlands, and hop gardens flanked by round and square kilns. A web of little lanes connects the villages and hamlets and beside one such secretive lane you find Shirkoak Farm, a Georgian farmhouse set in 8 acres of lawns with duck pond, tennis court, and billiards in the barn. Inside it is spacious and comfortable, and Tessa and Michael encourage you to make yourself at home, giving you a front-door key so that you can come and go as you please. The inviting drawing room with its open fire is yours to enjoy. Bedrooms, each with an en-suite bath or shower room, are thoughtfully and comfortably furnished. Two large but very friendly, well-behaved dogs, Natasha and Amber, love to accompany guests on strolls round the garden. A car is essential for touring this quiet rural area. It's an ideal spot for visiting the gardens at Sissinghurst, exploring Leeds Castle, and visiting historic Canterbury. The Channel Tunnel and Dover ferries are about a half-hour drive away. *Directions:* Leave the M20 at junction 9 and follow signs to Ashford. At the first roundabout take the A28 towards Tenterden for 5 miles. Turn left at the signpost for Woodchurch and after 2½ miles you find Shirkoak Farm on your right.

SHIRKOAK FARM
Owners: Tessa & Michael Leadbeater
Woodchurch, near Ashford
Kent TN26 3PZ, England
Tel: (01233) 860056, Fax: (01233) 861402
Email: shirkoakfarm@aol.com
3 rooms
£25–£27.50 per person
Open all year, Credit cards: MC, VS
Children over 10, No-smoking house
www.karenbrown.com/england/shirkoak.html

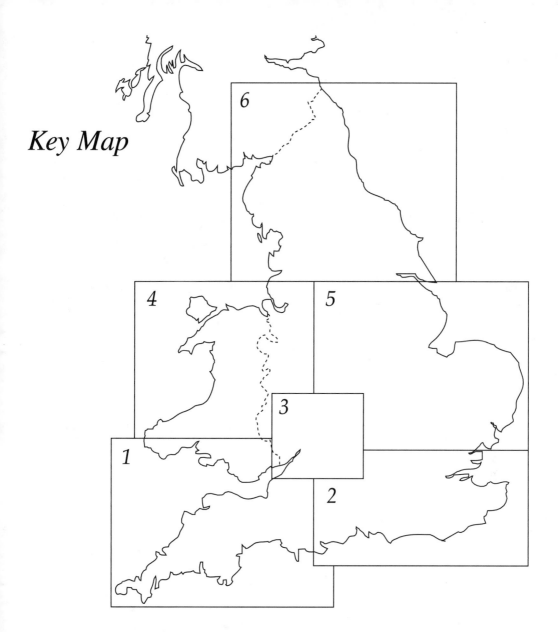

Key Map

6

4

5

3

1

2

175

Map 1

Map 2

Hornton

Broad Campden

CAMBRIDGE

Lavenham

Linton

Little Waldingfield

IPSWICH

Stoke-by-Nayland

Higham

Great Rissington

Thorington Street

Dedham

OXFORD

Colchester

M1

A1

M11

M40

M25

Henley

Maidenhead

M4

LONDON

Rushall

M3

M25

M25

M20

M2

Canterbury

Upper Clatford

Chiddingfold

Hadlow

Frant

Frittenden

Cranbrook

Winchester

Rogate

Petworth

M23

Horsted Keynes

Etchingham

Woodchurch

SOUTHAMPTON

Chilgrove

Wisborough Green

East Hoathly

Warehorne

Peasmarsh

M27

Storrington

Isfield

Battle

Rye

Wartling

BRIGHTON

PORTSMOUTH

ENGLISH CHANNEL

● Places to Stay
○ Orientation
✈ Airport

a	b
c	d

Quadrants

177

Map 3

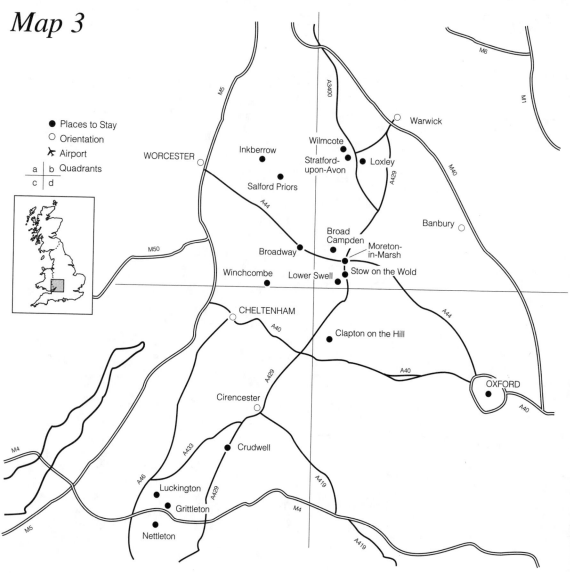

- ● Places to Stay
- ○ Orientation
- ✈ Airport

a	b	Quadrants
c	d	

WORCESTER ○

Inkberrow ●

Wilmcote ●

Stratford-upon-Avon

● Loxley

Warwick ○

M6

M1

M5

A3400

M40

A429

Salford Priors ●

Banbury ○

Broad Campden ●

Broadway ●

Moreton-in-Marsh ●

M50

A44

Winchcombe ●

Lower Swell ●

Stow on the Wold ●

CHELTENHAM ○

A40

Clapton on the Hill ●

A429

A44

OXFORD ●

A40

A40

Cirencester ○

M4

A433

Crudwell ●

A419

A46

A429

M4

Luckington ●

Grittleton ●

Nettleton ●

M5

A419

Map 4

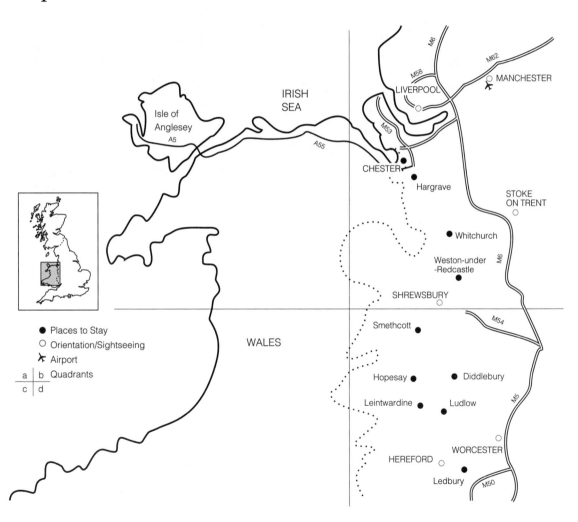

IRISH SEA

Isle of Anglesey
A5

A55

M6

M58

M62

LIVERPOOL

MANCHESTER

M53

CHESTER

• Hargrave

STOKE ON TRENT

• Whitchurch

Weston-under -Redcastle •

M6

SHREWSBURY

M54

WALES

Smethcott •

Hopesay •

• Diddlebury

M5

Leintwardine

• Ludlow

WORCESTER

HEREFORD

• Ledbury

M50

● Places to Stay
○ Orientation/Sightseeing
✈ Airport

a	b
c	d

Quadrants

179

Map 5

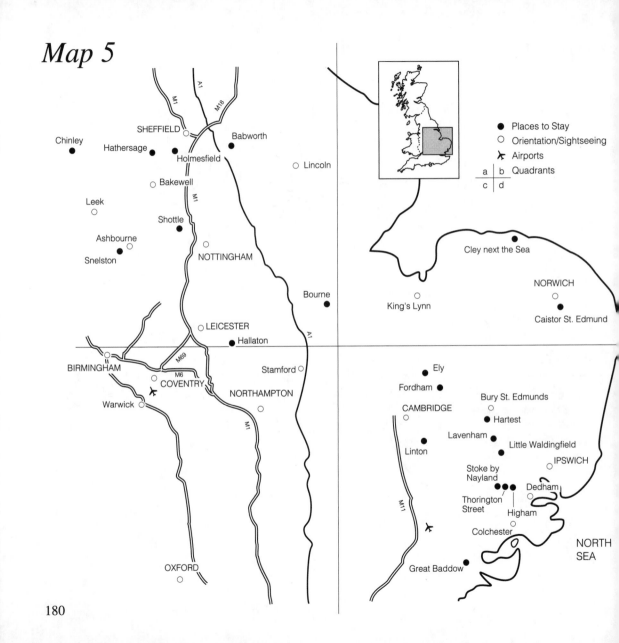

Places to Stay ●
Orientation/Sightseeing ○
Airports ✈

a	b	Quadrants
c	d	

Chinley ●
Hathersage ●
SHEFFIELD ○
Holmesfield ●
Babworth ●
Lincoln ○
Bakewell ○
Leek ○
Shottle ●
Ashbourne ○
Snelston
NOTTINGHAM ○
Bourne ●
King's Lynn ○
Cley next the Sea ●
NORWICH ○
Caistor St. Edmund ●
LEICESTER ○
Hallaton ●
BIRMINGHAM ✈
COVENTRY ○
Stamford ○
NORTHAMPTON ○
Warwick ○
Ely ●
Fordham ●
Bury St. Edmunds
CAMBRIDGE ○
Hartest ●
Lavenham ●
Little Waldingfield ●
Linton ●
IPSWICH ○
Stoke by Nayland ●
Dedham ○
Thorington Street ●●
Higham ○
Colchester ○
Great Baddow ●

NORTH SEA

Map 6

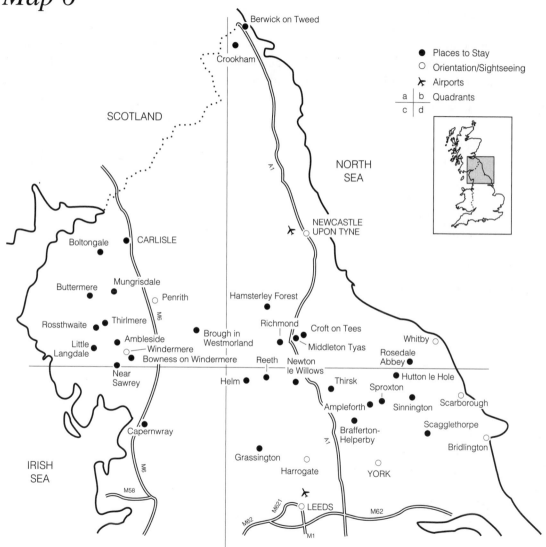

Berwick on Tweed

Crookham

SCOTLAND

A1

NORTH SEA

Places to Stay
Orientation/Sightseeing
Airports
Quadrants

| a | b |
| c | d |

NEWCASTLE UPON TYNE

Boltongale   CARLISLE

Buttermere   Mungrisdale   Penrith

Hamsterley Forest

Rossthwaite   Thirlmere   M6

Richmond   Croft on Tees

Little Langdale   Ambleside   Brough in Westmorland   Middleton Tyas   Whitby

Windermere   Bowness on Windermere   Reeth   Newton le Willows   Rosedale Abbey

Near Sawrey   Helm   Thirsk   Hutton le Hole

Sproxton

Ampleforth   Sinnington   Scarborough

Capernwray   Brafferton-Helperby   Scagglethorpe

IRISH SEA   M6   Bridlington

Grassington   Harrogate   YORK

M58

M621   LEEDS   M62

M62

M1

Places to Stay with Handicap Facilities

We list below all the places to stay that have ground-floor rooms or rooms specially equipped for the handicapped. Please discuss your requirements when you call your chosen place to stay to see if they have accommodation that is suitable for you.

Babworth, The Barns
Bath, Holly Lodge
Bath, Somerset House
Battle, Fox Hole Farm
Bourne, Cawthorpe Hall
Broad Campden, The Malt House
Buttermere Valley, New House Farm
Cley next the Sea, Cley Mill Guest House
Croft on Tees, Clow Beck House
Crookham, The Coach House
Frittenden, Maplehurst Mill
Hargrave, Greenlooms Cottage
Hartest, The Hatch
Loxley, Loxley Farm
Mungrisdale, The Mill Hotel
Near Sawrey, Ees Wyke Country House Hotel
Near Sawrey, Sawrey House
Oxford, Cotswold House
Petworth, The Old Railway Station
Reeth, The Burgoyne Hotel
Richmond, Whashton Springs Farm
Shottle, Dannah Farm
Storrington, Lime Chase
Thirlmere, Dale Head Hall

Thorington Street, Nether Hall
Upper Clatford, Malt Cottage
Wells, Beryl
Wilmcote, Pear Tree Cottage

Index

Index

Index   189

Join the Karen Brown Club

Why become a Karen Brown Club member? Savings! In no time at all members earn back their membership fee—in most cases, when they use just *one* of our membership discounts. Visit the Karen Brown website, *www.karenbown.com,* for details.

Karen Brown online store discount
A members-only discount worth an **additional 20%** off all orders in our store.

New discoveries: See our new hotels & B&Bs for next year as we find them
Receive early access to our newly discovered properties. If you cannot find a room in one of our currently recommended properties, these yet-to-be-published gems might be able to offer you alternative accommodation—a priceless benefit!

Discounts negotiated through our travel partners
Partners include participating recommended properties, such as Karen's own Seal Cove Inn. Benefits include condo rental upgrades in Mexico, airline discounts, auto rental discounts, and more!

A complete listing of member benefits can be found on our website:

www.karenbrown.com

Become a Member Today

Enhance Your Guides

Online

www.karenbrown.com

- Hotel News
- Currency Converter
- Corrections & Edits
- Meals, Wheels & Deals
- Links to Hotels & B&Bs
- Prints of our Favorite Covers
- Color Photos of Hotels & B&Bs

Visit Karen's Market

books, maps, itineraries,
and travel accessories
selected with our
KB travelers in mind.

Join the Karen Brown Club Online
Member benefits include an additional 20% discount in our
online store, access to new discoveries, special deals
negotiated with our travel partners, and more!

DISTINGUISHED INNS OF NORTH AMERICA

Publishers of the best travel guide to nearly 400 of the finest country inns, B&Bs, and unique small hotels in North America.

Now, more than ever, the traveling public needs places where gracious hospitality and comfortable and uncomplicated settings provide a respite from daily life and its tensions. Select Registry…where the destination becomes part of the journey.

Please visit our web site at **www.selectregistry.com** or call **1-800-344-5244** and tell us that you saw this message in your Karen Brown Guidebook. We will send you a complimentary copy of the registry ($15.95 retail) for just $3.00 postage and handling.

SHARE YOUR COMMENTS AND DISCOVERIES WITH US

Please share comments on properties that you have visited. We welcome accolades, as well as criticisms.

Also, we'd love to hear about any hotel or bed & breakfast you discover. Tell us what you liked about the property and, if possible, please include a brochure or photographs. We regret we cannot return photos.

Owner _____ Hotel or B&B _____

Address _____ Town _____ Country _____

Comments on places that are in the book and/or recommendations for your own *New Discoveries.*

Your name _____ Street _____

Town _____ State _____ Zip _____ Country _____

Tel _____ E-mail _____ Date _____

Do we have your permission to electronically publish your comments on our website? Yes _____ No _____

If yes, would you like to remain anonymous? Yes ___No ___, or may we use your name? Yes___ No___

Please send report to: Karen Brown's Guides, Post Office Box 70, San Mateo, California 94401, USA
tel: (650) 342-9117, fax: (650) 342-9153, e-mail: karen@karenbrown.com, www.karenbrown.com

SHARE YOUR COMMENTS AND DISCOVERIES WITH US

Please share comments on properties that you have visited. We welcome accolades, as well as criticisms.

Also, we'd love to hear about any hotel or bed & breakfast you discover. Tell us what you liked about the property and, if possible, please include a brochure or photographs. We regret we cannot return photos.

Owner _____ Hotel or B&B _____

Address _____ Town _____ Country _____

Comments on places that are in the book and/or recommendations for your own *New Discoveries.*

Your name _____ Street _____

Town _____ State _____ Zip _____ Country _____

Tel _____ E-mail _____ Date _____

Do we have your permission to electronically publish your comments on our website? Yes _____ No _____

If yes, would you like to remain anonymous? Yes ___No ___, or may we use your name? Yes___ No___

Please send report to: Karen Brown's Guides, Post Office Box 70, San Mateo, California 94401, USA
tel: (650) 342-9117, fax: (650) 342-9153, e-mail: karen@karenbrown.com, www.karenbrown.com

auto🜨europe®

Karen Brown's

Preferred Car Rental Service Provider

When Traveling to Europe
for

International Car Rental Services

Chauffeur & Transfer Services

Prestige & Sports Cars

Motor Home Rentals

800-223-5555

Be sure to identify yourself as a Karen Brown Traveler.
For special offers and discounts use your
Karen Brown ID number 99006187.

KB Travel Service

❖ **KB Travel Service** offers travel planning assistance using itineraries designed by *Karen Brown* and published in her guidebooks. We will customize any itinerary to fit your personal interests.

❖ We will plan your itinerary with you, help you decide how long to stay and what to do once you arrive, and work out the details.

❖ We will book your airline tickets and your rental car, arrange rail travel, reserve accommodations recommended in *Karen Brown's Guides,* and supply you with point-to-point information and consultation.

Contact us to start planning your travel!

800.782.2128 or e-mail: info@kbtravelservice.com

Service fees do apply

KB Travel Service
16 East Third Avenue
San Mateo, CA 94401 USA
www.kbtravelservice.com

Independently owned and operated by Town & Country Travel
CST 2001543-10

Seal Cove Inn

Located in the San Francisco Bay Area

Karen Brown Herbert (best known as author of the Karen Brown's guides) and her husband, Rick, have put 23 years of experience into reality and opened their own superb hideaway, Seal Cove Inn. Spectacularly set amongst wild flowers and bordered by towering cypress trees, Seal Cove Inn looks out to the distant ocean over acres of county park: an oasis where you can enjoy secluded beaches, explore tidepools, watch frolicking seals, and follow the tree-lined path that traces the windswept ocean bluffs. Country antiques, original watercolors, flower-laden cradles, rich fabrics, and the gentle ticking of grandfather clocks create the perfect ambiance for a foggy day in front of the crackling log fire. Each bedroom is its own haven with a cozy sitting area before a wood-burning fireplace and doors opening onto a private balcony or patio with views to the park and ocean. Moss Beach is a 35-minute drive south of San Francisco, 6 miles north of the picturesque town of Half Moon Bay, and a few minutes from Princeton harbor with its colorful fishing boats and restaurants. Seal Cove Inn makes a perfect base for whale-watching, salmon-fishing excursions, day trips to San Francisco, exploring the coast, or, best of all, just a romantic interlude by the sea, time to relax and be pampered. Karen and Rick look forward to the pleasure of welcoming you to their coastal hideaway.

Seal Cove Inn • 221 Cypress Avenue • Moss Beach • California • 94038 • USA
tel: (650) 728-4114, fax: (650) 728-4116, e-mail: sealcove@coastside.net, website: sealcoveinn.com

KAREN BROWN wrote her first travel guide in 1976. Her personalized travel series has grown to sixteen titles which Karen and her small staff work diligently to keep updated. Karen, her husband, Rick, and their children, Alexandra and Richard, live in Moss Beach, a small town on the coast south of San Francisco. They settled here in 1991 when they opened Seal Cove Inn. Karen is frequently traveling, but when she is home, in her role as innkeeper, enjoys welcoming Karen Brown readers.

CLARE BROWN, CTC, was a travel consultant for many years, specializing in planning itineraries to Europe using charming small hotels in the countryside. The focus of her job remains unchanged, but now her expertise is available to a larger audience—the readers of her daughter Karen's country inn guides. When Clare and her husband, Bill, are not traveling, they live either in Hillsborough, California, or at their home in Vail, Colorado, where family and friends frequently join them for skiing.

JUNE BROWN'S love of travel was inspired by the *National Geographic* magazines that she read as a girl in her dentist's office—so far she has visited over 40 countries. June hails from Sheffield, England and lived in Zambia and Canada before moving to northern California where she lives in San Mateo with her husband, Tony, their daughter Clare, their German Shepherd, and a Siamese cat.

BARBARA TAPP, the talented artist who produces all of the hotel sketches and delightful illustrations in this guide, was raised in Australia where she studied in Sydney at the School of Interior Design. Although Barbara continues with freelance projects, she devotes much of her time to illustrating the Karen Brown guides. Barbara lives in Kensington, California, with her husband, Richard, their two sons, Jonothan and Alexander, and daughter, Georgia.

JANN POLLARD, the artist responsible for the beautiful painting on the cover of this guide, has studied art since childhood, and is well-known for her outstanding impressionistic-style watercolors which she has exhibited in numerous juried shows, winning many awards. Jann travels frequently to Europe (using Karen Brown's guides) where she loves to paint historical buildings. Jann lives in Burlingame, California, with her husband, Gene.

Travel Your Dreams • Order Your Karen Brown Guides Today

Please ask in your local bookstore for Karen Brown's Guides. If the books you want are unavailable, you may order directly from the publisher. Books will be shipped immediately.

_____ *Austria: Charming Inns & Itineraries* $19.95

_____ *California: Charming Inns & Itineraries* $19.95

_____ *England: Charming Bed & Breakfasts* $18.95

_____ *England, Wales & Scotland: Charming Hotels & Itineraries* $19.95

_____ *France: Charming Bed & Breakfasts* $18.95

_____ *France: Charming Inns & Itineraries* $19.95

_____ *Germany: Charming Inns & Itineraries* $19.95

_____ *Ireland: Charming Inns & Itineraries* $19.95

_____ *Italy: Charming Bed & Breakfasts* $18.95

_____ *Italy: Charming Inns & Itineraries* $19.95

_____ *Mid-Atlantic: Charming Inns & Itineraries* $19.95

_____ *New England: Charming Inns & Itineraries* $19.95

_____ *Portugal: Charming Inns & Itineraries* $19.95

_____ *Spain: Charming Inns & Itineraries* $19.95

_____ *Switzerland: Charming Inns & Itineraries* $19.95

Coming soon: Karen Brown's *Pacific Northwest* and Karen Brown's *Mexico*

Name _____ Street _____

Town _____ State_____ Zip _____ Tel _____

Credit Card (MasterCard or Visa) _____ Expires: _____

For orders in the USA, add $5 for the first book and $1 for each additional book for shipment. Overseas shipping (airmail) is $10 for 1 to 2 books, $20 for 3 to 4 books etc. CA residents add 8% sales tax. Fax or mail form with check or credit card information to:

KAREN BROWN'S GUIDES
Post Office Box 70 • San Mateo • California • 94401 • USA
tel: (650) 342-9117, fax: (650) 342-9153, e-mail: karen@karenbrown.com, www.karenbrown.com